PRAISE FOR 'REASONS TO LIVE: ONE MORE DAY, EVERY DAY'

"Your book is going to help — and has helped — so many people. It will continue to augment destinies forever, and that's a beautiful thing. You should be proud of that."

Kevin Hines
Global suicide prevention speaker &
award-winning documentary filmmaker

"A remarkable book. I was especially moved by your own story… The power of stories to shine a light on suffering and redemption is well known, but it takes great courage and determination to capture and release them into the world in a way that builds the momentum for understanding and change."

Professor Patrick McGorry
Professor of Youth Mental Health (University of Melbourne),
Executive Director of Orygen, & Founding Director of Headspace

"Reasons to Live One More Day, Every Day is a book that is long overdue. In a world of political and personal fracture, where hope can often seem in short supply, Reasons to Live offers just that, through the narratives of 10 people whose honest and raw accounts show that there is a way through, that help can be found, and love for life restored. This book could save lives."

Melinda Tankard Reist
Author, speaker, co-founder Collective Shout:
for a world free of sexploitation.

"Jas, these stories, including yours, are incredibly powerful. Your heart to shine a light on such painful experiences is incredible and I wholeheartedly champion you as you continue to bring really tough topics into everyday conversation. The stigma that has been attached to mental illness for far too long is being removed one powerful story at a time in this book."

Renee Chopping
International Aftercare Director,
Destiny Rescue International

'**Stories sourced in love**, where you can't help but feel oneness and unity with the individual, and with humanity."

Fiona Berkin
CEO, Destiny Rescue Australia

@Reasons to Live One More Day Every Day
For copies of any of the books in Jas Rawlinson's 'Reasons to Live' series, head to: www.jasrawlinson.com

REASONS TO LIVE
ONE MORE DAY, EVERY DAY

VOLUME 2

Remarkable true stories of hope,
resilience, and triumph over adversity

JAS RAWLINSON

Reasons to Live: One More Day, Every Day
Remarkable true stories of hope, resilience, and triumph over adversity
© Jas Rawlinson 2019

All rights reserved. No part of this publication may be reproduced, stored in a retrieval system, or transmitted in any form or by any means, electronic, mechanical, photocopying, recording or otherwise, without the prior written permission of the author.

ISBN: 978-1-925935-76-9 (paperback)
        978-1-925935-84-4 (eBook)

 A catalogue record for this book is available from the National Library of Australia

Cover Design: Islam Farid
Design and Typeset: Ocean Reeve Publishing
Printed in Australia by Ocean Reeve Publishing

Published by Jas Rawlinson and Ocean Reeve Publishing
www.oceanreevepublishing.com

Dedication

I would not be the woman I am today, without an army of incredible people who've surrounded me. In particular, this book is dedicated to my family — whose support has been unwavering through every dark period in my life — and especially to our son. 'R,' may you grow up with a deep understanding of the value you bring to this world, and above all, that no matter how tough life gets, there are so many reasons to dig deep and keep putting one foot in front of the other. We've got your back kiddo, and you're never alone.

Content Warning

The following stories are powerful and personal accounts of each individual's unique life journey, and therefore may contain triggering subject matter (including discussions around suicide attempts and recovery). Please be aware that the information contained in this publication (including the resource section) is not recommended as a substitute for professional support. Should any of the content in this publication trigger feelings of distress, please seek professional support from your GP, or Lifeline (13 11 14).

Contents

Foreword: Patrick McGorry xi
The Story Behind Reasons to Live xiii

Surviving & Thriving After Childhood Trauma 1
   A note from Jas Rawlinson 3
   Prema Ra 5
   David Harris 19
   Jenn Murray 29
   Fai 39

Surviving & Thriving with Bipolar Disorder 49
   A note from Jas Rawlinson 51
   Jason Rantall 53
   Ashlee Reid 65
   Special Feature: Kevin Hines 77

Surviving & Thriving After Sexual or Domestic Violence 83
   A note from Jas Rawlinson 85
   Laura 87
   Angela McFarlane 101

Surviving & Thriving with Chronic Illness 113
   A note from Jas Rawlinson 115
   Justine Watson 117

Resources 133
    Get the Facts 135
    Jas Rawlinson's Hand-Picked Mental Health Warriors 141
    Professional Support Contacts 145

Acknowledgements 147
Author Bio 149
Connect With Jas 151

Foreword: Patrick McGorry
(Founding Headspace Director)

The toll wrought by mental illness in Australia is enormous, and the tip of this iceberg is the rising rate of suicide in our country — with eight people dying every single day. Even though mental illness has the greatest impact of all health conditions on our society, it remains seriously neglected with most Australians affected unable to access high quality care.

I was first inspired to enter the field of psychiatry as a young doctor, after witnessing the serious neglect of people with mental illness. In my 38 years in mental health, I have seen a series of innovations and positive developments, however these are merely oases of enlightenment, and ultimately, our health system has failed to treat people who experience mental illness with the same seriousness and skill that it offers to those with physical illness.

Throughout my career, my focus has been to create much more holistic and optimistic cultures of care which can deliver early intervention and better outcomes, especially for young people. These include early psychosis programs, Orygen's specialist youth mental health services and research program, and of course Headspace, which is now in well over 100 Australian communities and saving lives and futures. In addition to a raft of new scientific evidence, the success of Headspace is heavily based upon youth engagement, and the voice of lived experience from young people and families. Until recently there has been a reluctance among mental health professionals and sections of the media to talk openly about lived experience and especially suicide. Fortunately, we have mostly transcended this fear; one which reinforced century-old taboos regarding suicide.

However, if we are to make real progress in reducing the heavy toll of suicide and disability on our society, we need to completely redesign our health system and fund mental health care in proportion to the need of the population, and to provide evidence-based care. This will require a financial model at *least* at the level of the NDIS or even greater. Further, a co-design approach with people who use the system is essential, as they are the greatest allies of reform-minded professionals like myself.

The power of stories to shine a light on suffering and redemption is well known, but it takes great courage and determination to capture and release them into the world in a way that builds momentum for understanding and change. Jas Rawlinson's own moving story of suffering and mental ill-health galvanised her to help others survive and flourish despite exposure to trauma, loss, and pain. The collection of stories of survival against the odds contains many lessons which will guide others and provide hope to all who face these crises and ordeals in life. It also reveals that the perpetrators of violence are often victims themselves; victims of undiagnosed mental illness — and of their own traumas and suffering — who are struggling in mortal combat with their own internal conflicts. Men with violent and abusive childhoods are a common example, and often have as few escape routes as the victims they harm or even kill. However, the dominant message in this book is one of triumph over adversity, of hope and resilience, and of the healing power of love and care for others.

For these reasons and more, I am honoured to be a part of a book such as 'Reasons to Live: One More Day, Every Day.' To all readers of this book, I wish you courage, hope, and strength from the brave stories inside these covers. You are valuable, life is precious, and you are meant to be here.

PATRICK MCGORRY AO
Professor or Youth Mental Health: University of Melbourne
Executive Director: Orygen, the National Centre of Excellence in Youth Mental Health
Founding Director: Headspace, the National Youth Mental Health Foundation

The Story Behind Reasons to Live

Jas Rawlinson

"For so many years after Dad died my coping mechanism was to downplay the seriousness of his suicide or just mentally file it away with an industrial-sized broom. As far as I was concerned, I didn't want to talk about it. I didn't need to talk about it... But then something changed. In one moment, I made a decision to go against everything I'd been doing for the past 13 years since his death. Instead, I decided to begin opening up about my life. That was where 'Reasons to Live' was born."

"Why write a book about suicide survivors and people who've experienced mental illness?"

It's a question I've grown used to answering over the past two years, since releasing the first volume of 'Reasons to Live.' It's also a question that's very understandable.

For some people, the topic of suicide is simply too traumatic to speak of; for others, it's seen as distasteful or 'not great dinner conversation.' When you couple this with the ongoing fear and stigma around discussing suicide, particularly by those within the media, then it's really no wonder so many people shy away from the topic!

Yet, according to the World Health Organisation, every year we lose around 800,000 people to the silent killer that is suicide. On average, that breaks down to more than 2000 lives lost per day.

Just take a moment to let that sink in; that's almost one million people per year, who are no longer with their loved ones. And when you stop to consider the friends and family impacted by the ripple effect of all those deaths? Well, from my experience, it's almost impossible to find a single soul who hasn't been impacted in some way by suicide.

The sad reality is, even with all the progress we've made as a society we still have a long way to go. As someone who grew up in a family environment of constant fear where I often felt suicide was the only way to escape my dad's mental abuse, and then lived through the guilt and trauma of losing my dad to suicide, I guess you could say I've experienced the issue of suicide in many different ways. On one hand, I know intrinsically what it's like to feel that there is no hope or purpose to life — and yet I also know how deeply the trauma extends to those left behind by a loved one's suicide.

For all of these reasons and more, suicide prevention and mental health awareness have become one of my main areas of focus in the last few years as a freelance writer and speaker. What people may not realise, however, is that no one is more surprised to see me talking about these issues than…well…me!

You see, as a child I was so chronically shy and filled with self-hatred that I couldn't even stand in front of my classmates and give a presentation without my hands shaking like a leaf and my voice cracking like that of a prepubescent boy. In fact, I was *so* anxious about public speaking that I actually cut a deal with one of my teachers so I wouldn't have to do my assignment in front of the class!

It's a memory I've reflected on a lot over the last few years, as I've spread the message of 'Reasons to Live' to more and more audiences around Australia. Every single time I walk onto a stage or stand in front of a crowd, I always experience this moment of surrealism where I think to myself: 'WTF. How did I get here?' Seriously, never in a million lifetimes did I ever think I'd be able to speak in front of an audience without my heart trying to tear itself out of my chest, while my stomach did its best impression of a rollercoaster. As for the thought of speaking about things like suicide? Well, as we Aussies like to say, 'Yeah, nah.'

The truth is, for so many years after Dad died my coping mechanism was to downplay the seriousness of his suicide or just mentally file it away with an industrial-sized broom. "Oh, he's not around," was my standard vague and breezy reply when people asked if I had a father. As far as I was concerned, I didn't want to talk about it. I didn't *need* to talk about. Nothing was going to change the past, right? And besides, living free of my dad's psychological abuse and terrifyingly violent tirades was all I really cared about.

But then something changed. In one moment, I made a decision to go against everything I'd been doing for the past 13 years since his death. Instead, I decided to begin opening up about my life. That moment transpired in 2016, during a long road trip to my home town of Coffs Harbour. It was late at night, I was four hours into my trip — and bored as hell — and as tends to happen, my mind began to wander. Somehow (call it coincidence or something divine) I found myself reflecting on how far I'd come in my 31 years of life. '*How on earth did I survive those early years?'* I thought, curiously. *'What was it that helped me keep afloat when the tidal waves of depression and suicidality threatened to drag me down? Why did I survive when so many others don't?'*

The more I reminisced that night, the more my heart ached at the thought of all those who had lost their will to live — particularly children and teens. To me, it didn't make sense that I had been able to break free of the darkness that had plagued me for so many years, while so many others did not. After all, there's nothing superhuman about me. Yet somehow, I had not only survived…but thrived. I'd found the tools to break free from my PTSD (following a sexual assault at age 20), and also silenced the voices of self-doubt that had manifested from so many years at the mercy of my dad's rage. On that night, as my mind jumped back and forth between hundreds of memories, I realised the answer to this question.

I survived because of two specific things: resilience, and a commitment to keep living one more day, and then doing it all again the next.

Was it easy? Shit no. There were so many times I felt too tired to keep on going; like at age 17, when my dad's rage and verbal abuse became more frequent and monstrous.

During those days, I spent countless hours scrawling diary notes about how much I wanted to die and how little anyone would care. Somehow, though, I kept kicking against the tidal waves of suicide, until the murky water receded and I was able to see dry land.

Coming out the other side of my dad's abuse, and his eventual suicide, felt like being dumped on a storm-littered shoreline after years at sea; traumatised and relieved; hopelessly lost yet finally safe.

Of course, my journey didn't end there. For those who've read my story in volume one of 'Reasons to Live', you'll know that there were many other hurdles, traumas, and struggles waiting for me. However, over time I was able to get through each one — primarily, by holding on to the following truth: *'If I've been able to survive every day up until now, then one day, this too will pass and I'll be on the other side of it.'*

Thankfully, those moments of relief did finally arrive, and I was able to start thriving instead of just surviving. But — as I said earlier — I never planned to talk about the awful, terrifying, traumatic things I'd survived. That kind of stuff is ugly and shameful, right? I mean, who would want to listen to such sad stories? (Or so I thought.)

However, as the years passed and I grew older, I discovered something interesting; namely, that so many of my friends had been through domestic or sexual violence as well. From close school mates and coworkers, to online friends, I soon discovered that nearly every woman I spoke to had a story of sexual harassment, rape, or abuse. Over time I realised that the things I had been carrying alone, all the ugly, embarrassing and 'raw' memories, were also embedded into the fabric of so many other people's lives.

With shocking clarity, I finally realised that I wasn't alone; that other people had walked this path too, and climbed bloody-footed and bruised out of the sea and up toward that lighthouse of 'Hope'. Yes, some of us emerged with subtle scars and locked-suitcases of trauma strapped to our backs, while others dragged themselves along with open wounds and broken limbs. Yet, each of us had survived and continued to keep striving for that lighthouse of safety.

For me, my journey to healing came in many different ways; in particular, volunteering. At the time I was in an emotionally unstable 'relationship' (if you could even call it that), I'd just gotten fired from my job in a bulk foods shop (because I'd asked for a few days off to volunteer at a festival), and I was facing the harsh reality of living off Centrelink or moving back in with my mum at age 26. (Which, let's face it, feels like a failure when you're in your mid 20s).

As it turned out, though, getting fired from that crappy job was the best thing that ever happened to me! (Also, let's be honest, I was only there for the sweet discounts anyway). Although it was hard to see at the time, this one moment later revealed itself as a defining moment in my journey. It became the catalyst to discovering my passion and purpose — writing and advocating for important social issues. Interestingly, my movement into the world of volunteering also transformed my emotional health in ways I never expected. As I've since discovered, not only does volunteering reduce stress and improve wellbeing, but it also creates a natural high. In fact, research and studies have found that up to 95% of volunteers report feeling happier and more emotionally well (Volunteers Australia, 2015).

In my experience, I found that volunteering not only got me out of my own damn head, but it also helped me discover who I really was at my core. Instead of looking to crappy relationships to fulfil me, I started thinking more about what I wanted out of life, what inspired me, and what I could *give* to others. With this change in mindset, I decided to stop moping around and instead make it my mission to squeeze as many adventures and soul fulfilling experiences as I could out of life. During those years I ran anti-human trafficking events, wrote music reviews for local punk and indie bands, photographed global superstars like John Mayer and Jason Mraz, helped paint a two story house in Thailand for a survivor of child-trafficking, dug trenches at a child exploitation prevention home, stripped out and cleaned houses after the Brisbane floods, and started writing about issues of social injustice for my blog 'Thoughts From Jas' — all while working a full time job. Was it exhausting at times? Yes, definitely. There were many nights where I despaired that the things which brought me the most fulfillment, didn't seem to pay very well (or were so hard to get a career in). But at the end of the day they gave me a sense of purpose and kept my mental health stable, and eventually, my relentless pursuit of creativity was rewarded. Finally, I got my foot in the door of my dream job.

Over the coming years I worked in a number of different writing jobs and roles, and also went on to co-found Brisbane's first domestic violence memorial. At that point, I still had no desire to talk about suicide. That is, until that night where I caught myself reminiscing about how much I'd experienced in life and how many lives have been lost to the beast that is suicide.

As I began to delve into the issue and our frightening suicide rates here in Australia, I began to discover something both terrifying and also comforting. You see, the more I started to share about my story with friends and acquaintances, the more I discovered that — just like domestic and sexual violence — nearly every person I spoke to had been touched in some way by the darkness of suicide. To me that was an issue worth talking about, and so, without any idea of what it would entail or how many brick walls I'd come up against (and there were many!), I began searching the country for trauma and suicide survivors. Over a period of 12 months, I spoke to people all across the country and helped them write their stories. The deeper I crawled through the rabbit hole, the more I realised that this was not just a journalistic project. This was my life calling. And there was no going back.

That was when 'Reasons to Live' was born.

It's now been three years since I started this journey into the world of mental health and suicide prevention awareness. It's a journey that has brought some of the most wonderful people into my life, and opened my eyes to stories and social issues that I would never have been aware of otherwise. Unfortunately, it has also opened my eyes to a lot of shocking and damaging attitudes from 'experts' and professionals within the suicide prevention field — many of whom have revealed their true nature as mere 'ladder climbers' who care only for their own pockets and status, rather than joining forces to stop suicides.

Nothing has really demonstrated this more to me, than the process of writing this second volume. In fact, at one point earlier this year I seriously began to doubt whether I should change the whole book to a much more censored and blasé version, as suggested to me by someone within a suicide prevention organisation.

'Maybe they're right,' I remember thinking to myself, as I paced the kitchen on a warm autumn morning. *'Maybe I shouldn't publish this book. Maybe it is dangerous to talk openly about people's past suicide attempts — even though they have risen above and rebuilt their lives.'*

On that day, as I looked at the red lines through my edits — stories that I had spent months working on in collaboration with several brave suicide survivors — I felt deep disappointment seeping into my heart; disappointment that people who had already been silenced so greatly through the shame and stigma of mental illness were now facing further stigma when they tried to speak out. Then came anger. *'Why even have campaigns encouraging people to speak out about their struggles, if only to tell them their stories are too raw'?* I thought. *'What's the point of putting a huge emphasis on recognising "lived-experience," if those who are survivors can't even use the word "suicide?"'*

Deep down, I believe that this person just wanted to do what they thought was best. But from my research and study, as well as the honest feedback I've received from suicide survivors and bereaved family members around the world, I've since realised that not only are these attitudes without evidence, but they are also outdated and dangerous. By continuing to silence and censor the voices of those who have survived and rebuilt their lives, we effectively ensure that those who are still struggling are cut off from the very voices that could get through to them (particularly, when campaigns and 'clinical speak' fail to).

As Kevin Hines shared with me earlier this year, during an interview we did together:

> "Talking about suicide in graphic detail and leaving the audience in pain, *is* dangerous. Leaving them in the painful struggle and saying nothing about how you found recovery, *is* dangerous. But talking about your attempt in some detail, while following up with recovery, tools and tricks, and physical resources to take home, *that* saves lives."

Some may say I'm taking a risk by helping suicide survivors to tell their stories. I'm sure there are a few organisations who will criticise my work, and even try to silence it (as they've done to several of my friends). At the end of the day, however, I'm okay with my decision to support the voices in 'Reasons to Live.' I'm prepared to go against the grain. Because I believe the only way we will truly make change is to elevate the voices of those who have walked through the fire, survived, transformed their pain into purpose, and can now speak hope into the lives of those still surrounded by the flames of despair. Are their stories 'pretty?' No. Do they sugar coat the facts? Definitely not. Do their stories change lives and give hope? *Absolutely!* These people have survived some of the most dark and difficult things you could possibly imagine, and yet they refuse to give in or be silenced. Instead, they choose to keep living one more day every day, and to spread the message: 'There is a way through the pain; there is a reason to live; we're in this together, and you're not alone.'

And with that said, I'd like to introduce you to 'Reasons to Live: One More Day, Every Day - Remarkable true stories of hope, resilience, and triumph over adversity.'

REASONS TO LIVE...
Surviving & Thriving After Childhood Trauma

A note from Jas Rawlinson

Across the globe, it is estimated that one in four adults have experienced physical abuse during their childhoods (WHO, 2016). When you take into consideration the 7.7 billion people in our world, that equates to *over 1 billion people.* And when you stop to think of how many more children have been subjected to neglect, or emotional and sexual abuse, you can see that we're really just dealing with the tip of the iceberg.

It's been said that if we could significantly reduce global rates of childhood trauma, many other social issues in our world would be drastically improved. Addiction, broken relationships, suicide, mental illness… So many of the issues impacting humankind today stem directly from childhood trauma. In fact, data from The Adverse Childhood Experiences (ACE) Survey, discovered that male children who met six or more categories in the ACE test, had a 4,600% increased likelihood of later becoming an injection drug user.

For these reasons, as well as my own personal experience with psychological childhood trauma, I felt it extremely important to give a platform to a survivor of child abuse in this second volume. Little did I know just how inundated I would be! Sadly, I could have filled an entire book with this single topic, because nearly every person who contacted me had a story to share of childhood trauma.

In the end, I decided on four brave survivors whose life journeys I felt gave a diverse and impactful understanding of how deeply devastating childhood trauma can be. More importantly, however, I chose those stories that would prove beyond any doubt, that no matter what you have experienced, there is always hope, and above all else, there is always a reason to live. These brave individuals are not defined solely by their childhood trauma, yet their experiences shine a much-needed light on this social injustice.

With that said, I'd like to introduce you to Prema, David, Jenn, and Fai.

Prema Ra
Byron Bay, NSW (Australia)

"I have chosen to make friends with my depression, and that has helped enormously. I listen with compassion to the stories my darkness has come to tell. I hear my suicidal wail as a song of overwhelm, and I cradle that wounded part with a willingness to sit with it — without judgement or recoil."

A note from Prema

This story is a tough gig. It wasn't easy to write. It isn't easy to read. I've left out all the horrible details, but even so, you may still find it hard to read at times. I have chosen to break my story up by telling it from three different perspectives and 'voices.' You'll notice that at times there will be a 'Narrator,' whose job it is to speak the most painful truths (and to give some commentary or perspective on the story). At other times, I will be writing in my own voice, telling the facts of the events as they unfolded, as well as in present time (these are the italic sections). I hope doing this eases you through the layers and stages of this story. At the end of the day, I'm not here to give anybody advice, or to fix anyone. I can only speak about what happened to me, and how I eventually found a way to 'love being alive.'

"Prema"

The colours of my first childhood house are clear in my mind. The 1950's puffed themselves up with a wild palette of hues; lime greens, salmon pinks and gunmetal greys (always with white trim). Blue hydrangeas grew freely along the front wall of the house, the burst of colour a sweet sight against the dull grey walls.

Four-year-old kids are not supposed to remember details like this; yet I remember it all. I could draw you a floor plan of the house and put all the furniture in, just as it was. All the places that he did it. The bath. The closed-in side verandah — not the back verandah. The bath. The red vinyl lounge chair. His bed. The shed out the back. The bath… I still remember the smell of him when he wanted me in that way. Yet we left that house, and that tiny town, when I was still so young.

You know how this story goes. I was one man's sex slave from the time I was three months old (yes, sadly there were witnesses) until I was 15. No time was safe. No place was safe. He was so brazen that there were many times when people were nearby as he was using me for his gratification. I still find it hard to believe that he was never caught.

I also remember his small silver pistol, which was kept concealed in his trouser pocket at all times. Late at night as he came into my bedroom, he would slowly and deliberately place the pistol on the bedside table, right next to my head. Never once did he say out loud that he would kill me; but in the silence of the dead of night, I knew exactly what he could do to me — whenever he felt like it.

With each and every one of my birthdays his demands escalated. It was his twisted idea of a 'birthday present.' Every moment I was with him was terrifying, but at least it wasn't every night. Once I turned nine, however, that changed.

The terror of living inside this daily hell drove me to become so desperate for a way out that, for the first time, my fear of speaking out was slightly less than my fear of what might come next. Just prior to my 10th birthday, I went to a local priest to ask for help. Through reluctant lips I forced the words out — the hardest words I've ever had to say. I didn't even know the proper terms to describe what was going on, but it didn't matter in the end. None of it mattered. The priest took me into the chapel. He walked me up between the rows of pews, and through to the altar. Beckoning me to follow, he then led me to the very back of the altar area and pulled aside a heavy red velvet curtain, revealing a hidden door. There, in the secret room, the priest made me do to him what I had been experiencing at home. Now I had two abusers to deal with!

Three months later, on a grey November day, the priest died in a car accident. My relief was huge. That whole experience of reaching out for help was so traumatic for me, though, that I did not reach out again for many years.

Solitary. Lonely. Sad.

Somehow, amidst the backdrop of the ongoing abuse, I managed to go to school. But I failed to thrive. Learning was difficult, and I could barely read and write all throughout primary school. On one occasion, I remember my teacher giving me an 'F-minus' for spelling; because apparently an 'F' did not reflect the extent of my inadequacy. I was nine years old. (And we know what was happening at that time).

The belief that I was stupid and hopeless began to take root, infiltrating my sense of self. It probably comes as no surprise, then, that I was also bullied relentlessly.

The room is hot. My school uniform sticks to my back as sweat soaks through the cloth. As the afternoon drags on, the classroom fills with murmuring and the restlessness in the room bounces from child to child. Unexpectedly, there is a loud knock on the heavy blue door. Abruptly it swings open, and with the presence of a sergeant major, 'she' strides across the room. "Lazy, Liar, and Rude; come to my office, IMMEDIATELY," she bellows, before disappearing as suddenly as she had arrived. I know what is going to happen in the Principal's office today — just like so many other days over the past few years. Slowly, hesitantly, I slither up from my chair and drag myself to the office, head bowed low and shoulders drooped... Defeated.

It was my teachers who bullied me the most. Back then they were allowed to do that. During those four years the principal only ever called me 'Liar.' Never once did she use my name. The canings with the metal strip ruler were regular and prolific — even though the kids all called me 'goody-two-shoes'. The year I turned eight was particularly brutal for canings, but then again, all the years at that school were brutal. And through it all, there were no friends to act as a distraction from my pain.

Solitary. Lonely. Sad.
Shy. Timid. Cowering.

"Narrator"

The ingredients for lifelong depression were all there, already entrenched. Her world was black with secrets and shame. The insatiable loneliness was an unbearable pain that drove a spike through her life. Yet, deeper than the imprint of all those horrid experiences, lay something else. Inside this terrified and tiny person beat the heart of a hero. When life offered her better, she did better.

As soon as she went to high school the bullying stopped, and that enabled many things to change for her. By the end of her first year in high school she had become a 'straight A' student. No one was more surprised than she! Finally, her niche had appeared. As she soon realised, being a nerd was the ticket out of hell she'd been waiting for. And so it was, that books became her friends. Yes, she was still solitary, lonely, sad, shy, timid, and cowering; but she was good at something. It helped.

Amidst the ongoing nightmare of her home life, she clung to this newfound sense of purpose. One day, she knew she would be free. For now, however, she had to protect herself. Every day she feared falling pregnant, so she hatched a plan. She was almost 12.

"Prema"

It's 5pm. 'Quick! He'll be home soon!' I grab the bread and butter from the fridge. Two slices — tonight's dinner. Two more slices — tomorrow's breakfast. I'm hurrying now. One slice of bread drops to the floor. Going too fast; no time to care. I quickly scoop it up and run the knife through the butter, begging it to spread faster. I tear holes in the bread as I hurry. No time to care. Urgently, I spread the Vegemite across the buttery mess. Good enough! 'Now, go to the bathroom right now — quickly, quickly!' I tell myself.

Back in my room I brace my back against the bed, and push with all my might, scrabbling as my feet slip on the carpet. With one last almighty shove I get it in place, blocking one of the doors from sliding open. 'Quickly, quickly! Get the other door locked!' Opening the wardrobe door hard against the wall, I use all my strength to jam a tennis racket between it and the sliding door. My legs buckle, and I sag to the floor with my back slumped against the bed. 'Ahhh,' I sigh. 'Safely locked in for the night.'

"Narrator"

She felt safe for a short while with this arrangement. Each morning she would get up in the dark, get dressed very quietly, and sneak silently out the back door. In the laneway that ran behind the house she found bushes that she could hide behind to empty her bladder. Then she would walk, in the darkness before morning's twilight, along the wide streets lined with tall, aged sycamore trees; all the way to the church about a mile away. There, she would wait for dawn to come — and later, for school to open. She lived on Vegemite sandwiches for that whole period.

Locked in her room night after night gave her time alone to process her thoughts. Sometimes she would write and write until all the emotion bled out. Other times, she'd draw images of dying by her own hand. She knew that so long as her hands were busy drawing, that they could not reach for the tools to do the deed. The next day she would burn all the pages; burning up the despair. She also wrote masses of poetry, thereby transmuting the pain into beauty — the great alchemy of words.

Sometimes he caught her sneaking out the back door. On those days, he would be very rough with her as punishment (you know what I am talking about). Then, one night, he found a way to dislodge the tennis racket using a stick. He was very rough with her that night too. She was at the brink, about to break.

Solitary. Lonely. Sad.
Shy. Timid. Cowering.
Desperate. Depressed. Defeated.

Relief was at hand, however. No longer young enough for 'his' needs anymore, she was sent far away to a school in Sydney. There, all alone in a big city, she felt safer than she had in her entire 15 years of life.

However, feeling safe was not enough to prevent murky thoughts from flooding her mind. She had been discarded — thrown away as an inconvenience. Those final years at school were like trying to tread water in a quicksand of suicidal depression. 'Hanging on by her fingernails, whilst dangling in the abyss,' is what she called it. The only thing that kept her alive was her fundamental belief that all murder was wrong — even her own. Back then, she had nothing else to keep her going. But it was just enough. And that was all she needed.

In those last two years of high school she was forced to change schools repeatedly, and as a result, had no classes for half her subjects. So, instead, she taught herself Mathematics, Ancient History, and English. She'd be embarrassed at me telling you this, but she topped the school in two of those very subjects.

In truth, then, it was against all odds that she got into university. In a way, that's when her life began. She had finally escaped 'his' tyranny. The rest of her life was hers, to craft and sculpt into her own shapes.

She was writing a new script for her life.
Strong. Curious. Determined.

"Prema"

It's five years after graduation. Click, buzz, whir! The sounds of the photo shoot are making my temples thump. My mouth is dry and my knees feel weak. It is my first time on TV. I've been teaching a lot since I became a physiotherapist and our profession needs a media liaison person. I am 'It,' apparently!

"Take two!" comes a shout from behind the spotlight. Thoughts run wildly through my mind and I take a deep breath. It is so good to feel my belly expand; to feel my nervous system calming. I spent this morning lecturing to 200 experienced

doctors, and here I am this afternoon in the TV studio. Even for me this is a big day! Actually, the more I think about it, the more excited I am.

"Action!" shouts the voice from behind the spotlight. A warmth that I don't immediately recognise floods through me and my breathing slows. I drop into my first taste of self-love.

The sounds of the cameras and the heat of the lights became familiar experiences over the years that followed. In short, my career had been a whirlwind of successful serendipity. I was a young woman in the early stages of my career, and yet I had already become the head physio in a big sports medicine clinic. My accountant joked that I was the most eligible woman in the city. So, almost by accident, I became quite wealthy. I worked hard (often too hard) and lectured extensively.

Let's not pretend that it was an easy ride to get to this point, though. My body had been crippled by the relentless torment that had filled my childhood for 15 years. My immune system had turned against me and attacked all my joints, and the arthritis was so severe that, by the time I was 19, I had to get around with the aid of two walking sticks.

I began my healing journey by first facing my fears in real life, rather than inside a therapist's office. I flung myself into a myriad of diverse life experiences, practised setting boundaries, and forged a self-care routine to nurture my body toward release and peace. Yoga, Tai Chi and swimming; weight training, walking and martial arts... Each served a purpose, and each helped me to claim my body as my own.

In time I learned that the greatest advantage I had in life was that I had experienced, first hand, many different kinds of pain — both mental and physical. This became a resource inside of me, especially when clients shared their extreme physical pain and the despair that came with it. Knowing another's pain as my own allowed me to reach out without judgement. My pain was rich with meaning and dense with purpose. Pain became a messenger, not an enemy.

Over time I became a wild adventurer into the core of my being. As I ventured into the heart of my deepest, murkiest depths, I was blessed to have some fabulous psychotherapists who travelled with me on those explorations. With their help, I was able to find my anger, which had been buried under mounds of shame and despair. The skillful guidance of my therapists showed me ways to express my anger, and release it, without harming myself or others. Conscious breathing became a great joy to me, and Feldenkrais Bodywork began to reprogram my nervous system toward calm and ease. At long last, I celebrated coming home to myself.

Day by day, I was finding a way to make peace with my past and keep moving forward. Life was no longer about just surviving, but more importantly, thriving.

Strong. Curious. Determined.
Active. Exploring. Expressing.

"Narrator"

With all that had come before and all that she had achieved, no one could have predicted what would happen next. In a surprising twist, at the height of her fame and fortune, she chose a whole other life for herself. Swapping her life of abundance and busyness, for one of silence and utter simplicity, she joined a 'hard school' Buddhist Monastery. Every day of the year, from 4am until 11pm, was (silently) the same; and for seven deeply dedicated years she meditated her butt off.

It was in the monastery that she learned how to live alongside her suicidal depression. She learned how to witness her thoughts and feelings without getting caught up in them, and she learned how to make friends with her pain. She flourished. As the thoughts emptied from her mind, the raw feelings could be seen, heard, and felt, as if for the first time. The ever-present demand for honesty within the monastery walls often elicited tentacles of fear that had lain hidden and unattended to, but there was nowhere to hide. So instead, she learned to face her fears as she had never faced them before. Slowly at first, and then more surely, courage grew, allowing her to face all the ways her terror had manifested within both mind and body.

At no time did she rush towards forgiveness. She knew she needed to feel, and to work through, the diverse emotions radiating outward from her horrendous childhood. Yet forgiveness did come, quietly and gently filling her heart and more, until it spilled over into her life.

Only then did she reprogram her nervous system to fully rest; to open and inhabit her body without recoil; to become capable of trust again. Trust is one of life's most daring endeavours.

After seven years she was told to leave the monastery and go and live her wisdom in the world.

Strong. Curious. Determined.
Active. Exploring. Expressing.
Honest. Open. Centred.

"Prema" — 'Listening is the loudest form of kindness

All that was half a lifetime ago. I have survived. I am an old lady now. I have lived the wisdom in my life to the best of my ability in each moment, even amidst life offering me many hardships, major illnesses, and financial destitution.

That doesn't mean that life has always looked pretty as I practised this wisdom. Far from it. It does mean, however, that I worked hard at not killing myself — no matter how much I wanted to end my life. In truth, there were years at a time where I hung over the precipice of suicidal craving, white knuckling it through each day; sometimes through each hour and each second. At the worst of times I'd sit in my car with both hands clamped hard on the steering wheel. I'd sit that way for hours, on the darkest and lowest days, knowing if my hands were gripping the steering wheel, then my hands could not reach for the tools to self-harm.

I have chosen to make friends with my depression and that has helped enormously. Today, I listen with compassion to the stories my darkness has come to tell. I hear my suicidal wail as a song of overwhelm, and I cradle that wounded part with a willingness to sit with it — without judgement or recoil. My darkness no longer has to scream at me as it leaps into the abyss, in order to get my attention. I listen to its whisper and I adjust my self-care routine to relieve the internal pressure. Medication and counselling also play a part, and I give myself permission — without shame or hesitation — to utilise them whenever it's appropriate.

At long last I have fallen in love with living; not by trying to fix myself or cure the depression, but rather by loving myself as I am. My hardships have definitely made me a better, deeper, and richer person. My compassion was a veneer really, until I was stripped of everything, through illness and dire poverty. Now my compassion has an aching depth that I cherish, because it connects me to life, to others, and to my core. Gratitude is the glue that binds my life into wholeness; I don't get out of bed until I've listed 10 things I'm grateful for!

It was impossible to guess that my life would be permeated with expansive belonging. When I least expected it, my life filled up to overflowing with the love of friends and family, all snuggled into a kind and loving community.

The bravery of brokenness has a brilliance within it, waiting to be found. I do not need to behave triumphantly, or force myself to live in a place of constant positivity. To *trust* is to *triumph*. To *dare to love* is a triumph. I honour those things on my sweet days and on the days that are bleak.

I love who I've become today. I'm so glad I stayed. I am who I am meant to be.

Grateful. Trusting. Growing…

PREMA RA is a physiotherapist who works exclusively with people who have long-term or complicated pain, and helps propel them forward on their journey to becoming well. In addition to surviving her childhood, and three serious suicide attempts in her twenties, Prema has also endured Encephalitis (an infection and inflammation of the brain) that left her barely able to speak, walk, or even remember her own name for the best part of a decade. She now finds gratitude in every little thing. 'All life is precious. Every word is a treasure. Each moment matters.' Find out more about her work on Facebook: @ Prema Ra's Vertebral Oscillation Therapy and Exercise.

David Harris
Gold Coast, QLD (Australia)

"It has been a year since I began the long and emotionally traumatic process of seeking compensation for my institutional abuse. What keeps me going through every obstacle, is the knowledge that the more I speak out about things I'm passionate about, like institutional sexual abuse and domestic violence, the more it encourages others to do so."

It was 1976, and I was a 17-year-old kid preparing for my school exams. Like many teenagers, I had a bit of a crush on one of my teachers. Since I was really focused on my studies though, I decided to have a chat to a psychologist and see if they had any tips for how I could get over my crush and focus on my exams. It was really all very innocent.

One afternoon as I walked home from the bus stop, I noticed a police car parked outside our house. It was a curious thing to see. Kind of like seeing a fire brigade truck outside a building with no fire. It just didn't really make sense. Stepping through the front doors, I began to wonder if maybe it had something to do with what I'd discussed with the psychologist. That was when I saw the officer standing beside my mother. Waiting for them to ask about my teacher crush, I stood silently. But the question never came. Instead, I was ordered out the front door and into the cop car. 'Get in, now!' was all he said. I didn't have time to shower or eat, I was just taken — literally. It all happened within a minute or less. As I sat in the backseat with my mother, shock and disbelief began to take over. At no point did the police ask me any questions or tell me what was happening. It was like a bad dream.

As we travelled kilometre after kilometre, I watched from the window as trees flew by. *Where are we going, what is happening?* I wondered. Eventually, the car pulled up outside a psychiatric clinic in NSW. There, over 100kms from home, I was dropped off and left by myself. No one told me why I was there, or what the 'crime' was that I'd supposedly committed. All they said was: "You have no legal rights." Even now, 43 years later, I still remember them repeatedly telling me: "We can do whatever we want, David."

Soon after my arrival, I was taken — confused and scared — into the clinic area by two female nurses. This was the moment, the place, that my life was forever changed. I was sexually assaulted; first in the shower and then in the toilet. My perpetrators were the two female nurses. It was intensely painful, both physically and emotionally.

This was the start of several torturous experiences. At night, a torch would be shone into my eyes (which led to sleeping issues after I left the clinic), and many times I was given electric shock treatment. Not only was it entirely inappropriate, but also deeply traumatic. Throughout the week, I was forced onto medication so strong that it slurred my speech, slowed down my body functions, and made it impossible for me to ask what was happening or why I was there.

After seven painful, traumatic, and lonely days, I was finally discharged. As I was prepared for release, a staff member looked at me coldly, stating: "Now, keep taking this medication, or you'll be straight back here, and the same things will be done to you again." There was a sincerity in their voice that was terrifying. "Tell anyone what happened to you here, and you'll be sexually assaulted and given electric shock therapy again," they added, for extra emphasis. It was blackmail of the most disgusting kind.

Terrified of being sent back, I had no choice but to do as they said. Understandably, taking the medication became a fearful and anxious daily experience.

That week in my life, as a 17-year-old boy, robbed me of my adolescence. Due to the medication, and the trauma experienced at the clinic, I was classified as 'permanently incapacitated'. I was an emotional zombie. Physically and mentally, the smallest of things became impossible. Communicating clearly with others, making friends, getting a job… It felt like everything had been ripped away from me.

Several years later, by pure luck, I came to realise the full extent of the injustices I suffered. You see, I had just decided to further my studies, and upon applying, I received a letter stating that I would need to see a psychiatrist to assess my 'condition.' This was the moment I learned the truth. Sitting before the psychiatrist, I listened in absolute shock as he delivered his professional diagnosis. "David, there's nothing wrong with you," he stated. "The diagnosis you were given in 1976 was wholly inaccurate. In fact, you should never have been sent to the clinic or put on this medication to begin with." The absolute rage and shock I felt was unbelievable! To know that my sexual assault and all the trauma that followed, could have been prevented if not for their 'mistake?' Well, it's hard to put into words how traumatic that moment of clarity was.

Immediately I stopped taking my prescriptions. But after so many years of being medicated, going 'cold turkey' led to massive headaches and other severe side effects — some of which lasted for years. I also needed speech therapy, and as a consequence of everything I'd been through, began to suffer from post-traumatic stress disorder. The shame was massive, and I was plagued by insomnia and regular nightmares. To this day, those nightmares still continue.

I think people sometimes fail to understand how far the tentacles of entrenched trauma extend into your everyday life. In over 40 years, I have not been able to have a single relationship — or even kiss a woman — due to the association between the sexual abuse I suffered, and the feeling that having a relationship — or even sex — would be painful. Even just the mention or thought of the word 'sex' is enough to trigger the trauma I suffered on that day.

Even after coming off the medication, I was unable to work for many years (even though I really wanted to). Given that I couldn't look anyone in the face, had no real friendships, and was unable to express any emotion, my work prospects were zero. So instead, I dedicated the next decade of my life to being a full-time carer for my mum. Sadly, it was an experience that was humiliating and painful for the both of us. One memory that sticks with me most, is the night I spent four hours trying to drag her on a mat from the toilet to the bed. I had no family support; not for the trauma I'd experienced, and not with caring for mum.

Not long after Mum died, I was the victim of a con artist who robbed me of a lot of money. Afterwards, I realised just how alone — how unprepared for life — I was. At this point, I truly wished I was dead. And so it was, that on my way home from church mass one day (ironically), I found myself standing on the footpath looking at the cars speeding by. Before I could change my mind, my feet were already stepping out from the safety of the sidewalk, and with purposeful intent, I walked directly in front of a car heading toward me. The fact that I am writing this today is a true miracle. I still have no idea how I made it to the other side of the road, or how the car avoided me. All I remember is standing safely on the other side...

The fact that I survived my suicide attempt made me realise I needed to speak to a counsellor. So, I decided to reach out. Yes, it was scary, but it was the first step to getting help, and I knew my life depended on it.

One of the suggestions shared with me by my counselor, was to become more involved in my community through volunteer work, and to spend more time with other people who had similar interests. It was very difficult at first but I took her advice, and the more I did this, the easier it became. Inspired by my counsellor's words of support, I eventually realised what I wanted to do; to begin training as a counsellor myself!

A huge turning point in my life came when, after nearly four decades, I decided to speak out publicly. On that day in May 2014, I stood before my college classmates, and for the first time, spoke about the sexual abuse and trauma I suffered at the psychiatric clinic. As I opened up, I was overwhelmed by emotion; I just cried, and cried, and cried. It was the first time I'd expressed emotion in 38 years! As my teacher and fellow students crowded around to offer their support, I felt a massive weight lift from my chest. Finally, I could speak my truth and be heard. *Finally.*

As overwhelming as it was, that one moment made a giant difference in my life journey; and I wasn't the only one who noticed. My friends could only shake their heads in disbelief as they watched the change in my character and personality from one day to the next. To be honest though, it was a strange feeling. Expressing myself after so many years felt very weird! In fact, I am still learning to express my emotions effectively. It certainly is a journey, that's for sure.

Two years later, in 2016, I was rocked by the news that a woman who had spent time at the clinic where I was tortured, had died under shameful circumstances. I was racked by guilt. 'If only I had spoken out earlier', I thought to myself, 'then maybe her death could have been prevented.' It was sometime after this that a number of people at my college — including my wonderful teacher — encouraged me to take action; to hold to account those who had tortured me so many years beforehand, and to seek compensation for the trauma I had been left with.

With their support, I made the decision to do just that — a decision that I knew was going to be tremendously hard but also important. It was incredibly painful having to re-experience the whole trauma of my time at the clinic, and the after effects, in graphic detail. I cried a lot. At one point, when explaining to the police about my experience (they wanted evidence and specific details), I felt as though I was being interrogated, or even regarded as the perpetrator! As painful as that was for me, at least it gave me an insight into what other sexual abuse victims go through when talking to police. And most importantly, all of this paved the way for what was to be the greatest day in my life: October 22nd, 2018. The day that the National Apology to Victims and Survivors of Institutional Child Sexual Abuse, was held at Parliament House in Canberra.

Standing in the crowd that day, surrounded by other survivors, showed that I was not alone; that I was believed and supported. One of the most touching moments that day, was watching Julia Gillard (who ordered the royal commission) speak with such passion that she received a standing ovation. The crowd was so moved, and at one point, a survivor knelt before Julia and kissed her feet in heartfelt thanks.

On that day there were many appalling stories shared. Several politicians mentioned that some priests and clergy had in the past raped innocent children, and then made them confess to the same priests for their so-called 'sins'. It was hard not to feel guilty while listening to such stories; after all, my horror was not nearly as bad as that of many other victims and survivors. In particular, I found it hard to listen to the level of abuse experienced by so many innocent children. At one point, I collapsed my head to my knees, unable to stop the sobs that escaped my body. The trauma experienced by so many people around me was overwhelming.

As I cried, a lovely lady beside me rested her head on my shoulder; it was a small but powerful act of comfort — probably the most beautiful experience of my life. No one has ever told me they loved me, and that moment was the nearest experience to love I've ever felt. Thank you, Liz, for showing me such kindness on that afternoon.

Another highlight from that day was when the National Apology Reference Group Chairman, Cheryl Edwardes, stood between Scott Morrison and Bill Shorten, holding their hands up high as those of us watching on turned and embraced those beside us. We were a sea of people, standing in the Great Hall, with our hands, with our warmth, with our love... And together, we cried. We all cried. But we were not alone in our experiences. This was above politics. Sincerity from everyone was clear and genuine.

As I left the Great Hall that day, I was suddenly overcome by emotion and collapsed to the floor. Other survivors helped me to my feet, but once outside on the lawn, I again collapsed. So did many others. The sheer impact of that day, of the event, was enormous. But as I sat with a helper and chatted, I also felt proud; proud and lucky to be one of the survivors and winners there that day. I placed ribbons on the memorial tree and dipped my hands in the water to represent a 'cleansing' of my past, and to go forward with my hands, body, mind, emotions, and soul renewed.

Afterwards I spoke with others, who until that day, I didn't even know existed. The 400 of us came from all over Australia. The support we gave to each other was more intense, beautiful, and deep than I could possibly have imagined. We exchanged contact details. Unknown strangers turned into the best of friends — all because of our special bond.

I'm proud to say I was part of that day. I'm proud that, on that day in October 2018, I cried more tears than I ever have before. After I flew home the next day, I cried for two hours, overwhelmed, and also determined to do all I can to prevent sexual abuse from happening in our institutions.

How do I feel about life now? I feel I am very lucky. I say that in one sense, because in 2017, I started playing Australian Rules Football for the first time in my life. Joining the local club meant that I had the chance to finally make some genuine, real, and wonderful friendships. In fact, I call my teammates my 'true family', as they are the ones who are always there to support me through tough times. They are prepared to do anything for me, and vice versa. When I kicked a goal in my first ever match, at the age of 58, it was a victory for our team and also a victory for those who conquer obstacles in life's path.

Yes, there are many things I still wish for my life, like a loving relationship and to work as a counsellor, and those things will happen in time. However, for now, what is far more important is that I continue to speak out against past and present institutional sexual abuse and domestic violence. I want to do all I can to prevent it from happening in the future.

I feel proud that I have overcome so much (including a gambling addiction), and that I've found many different tools to help me on my journey. Coming to understand that I can still have my own relationship with God, even since walking away from the Catholic Church after decades of faithful service, has also been incredibly healing. With everything that has come to light in recent years, there are so many people out there who are struggling with deep hurt at the hands of the church, and I think it's so important for people to know that they can still continue their faith in whatever way they wish.

I've also discovered a love for running, and have since completed over seven marathons. Considering that many people don't even have the ability to walk or run, I feel very blessed to be able to enjoy such a sport. Once a week I care for the elderly, and I also spend time with friends at a public speaking group (another passion of mine). Keeping busy with things that make me feel alive, or help me give back to others, also helps a lot.

Meaningful face-to-face communication is far healthier, in every aspect, than communicating with images through social media. I think this is why I spend so much time volunteering or giving back to others. When you treat yourself and others with respect, when you have face-to-face communication with real people, when you smile, laugh, and learn to regard the past and its mistakes as opportunities to learn from, that is when you truly win in this game of life.

It has been a year since I began the long and emotionally traumatic process of seeking compensation for my institutional abuse. But regardless of the outcome, how can you put a financial figure on the destruction of your adolescence, lost relationships and career opportunities, and almost four decades of emotional numbness? Truly, there is no monetary amount that can reverse what I have experienced. I can only hope for justice and for a formal acknowledgment of the horrors done to me.

What keeps me going through every obstacle, is the knowledge that the more I speak out about things I'm passionate about, like institutional sexual abuse and domestic violence, the more it encourages others to do so. The words, 'Stop domestic violence always,' are painted on my front steps, and it is my hope that those passing by might see those words and think about what they can do to make a difference as well.

Those who were responsible for the sexual abuse, the rapes, the torture and floggings of so many of us around the world, must be held accountable. And not only the perpetrators, but also those who condoned the abuse; those who ignored it.

This is no time for silence. And now that I've found my voice, I will never be silenced again.

Some final words from David....

When I felt suicidal, I felt an overwhelming sense of despair
There seemed to be no remedy, my life was beyond repair
During such times I felt so alone
No one to connect to, no one to phone
I found it hard to sleep and to eat
Struggling through each day was a painful feat
There seemed to be no hope, I could not cope
Unless you have been through such times, you cannot know
Suicide loomed as an escape from my mist
I was checkmated in life's game of chess
Although so close to suicide, I did survive
I realised I had to call the crisis line
They listened to me with understanding and care
I realised that in time, I would not only cope but thrive
I sought help and made progress day by day
It sure wasn't easy, let me say
I made attempts to meet new people, to make friends
I'm so proud of doing that, for making amends
I am not alone, there is always hope
And suicidal? Pick up the phone; you (we) can cope.

> *DAVID HARRIS is an avid poet, and the author of the book: 'Living Your Life Through Verse'. In his spare time, he enjoys training for marathons and giving back to those in his community through random acts of kindness. As of 2019, David is still seeking financial compensation for the sexual abuse and psychological trauma suffered in 1976. To find out more about David's book, visit: inhousebookstore.com.au.*

Jenn Murray
Pittsburgh (United States)

"As a young child and teen, life was about surviving. But now, it's so much more. I'm a woman who is finally living with purpose — and thriving."

My life prior to 2011 was incredibly dark and different from what it is now. Very few know of what those years were like, and to be honest, I haven't shared much of that time with anyone. But I feel that it's time to tell my story.

As a little girl, life began in a thick, suffocating fog of hopelessness and depression; most of which centred around my father's abuse. For reasons I'll never know, he made the decision early on that I was going to be the child he despised. Consequently, his sole aim was to make my life as miserable as possible. I don't know how old I was when I first began to notice the emotional and verbal abuse, but from that tender age of awareness it was always there. Anything he could do to make me feel stupid, unworthy, disappointed, or frustrated, brought him a sickening amount of delight.

Every day was different, and my father's cruelty played out in a variety of ways. While some of the torture was 'in-the-moment,' other acts were cold and calculated. For example, he purposely turned my own sisters against me. This happened mostly due to the fact that my mother had begun working part-time and was sometimes absent during dinner.

As my father and my two younger sisters and I sat around the dinner table, he'd purposely encourage them to join in with his verbal abuse towards me. It was just one way in which he pointedly made things as awful as possible.

Anything — and everything — was a weapon to be used against me. But it wasn't just about humiliation; he also liked playing with my emotions. It was common for my father to get me excited about something, only to rip my dreams out from underneath me. One of the most hurtful instances of this occurred after my dad started letting me ride on his motorcycle with him. After seeing how much I *loved* going out on the bike, he promised that if I could save up enough money, I could buy my own helmet. I was *so* excited, and from that moment on I started saving every dollar ($50 was a lot for a child in the 1990s). When I finally reached my goal, he took me on a special father and daughter trip to select and buy my first helmet. I couldn't wait to start riding!

And then, it happened; the climax to his cruel plan. You see, now that I had the helmet — now that I'd saved and spent all my money — he was no longer interested in letting me ride. I kept pleading with him, over and over, but it was no use. I vividly remember the moment I finally gave up. I was standing in the garage watching my father get ready to go on a ride, when he finally turned and looked at me. "You can't go! Stop asking me," he sneered before riding off. I never asked again. Lonely and unused, my helmet sat on the garage shelf — a reminder of how much my dad hated me.

During my childhood, it felt as if my father was this constant force, always pushing me down. As a kid, I was naturally well-behaved, cheerful, and trusting. I was smart, creative, and did well in school. But none of that mattered to my father. Of course, he was more than okay with my sisters. He treated them just fine. But me? Nothing but cruelty and abuse.

Needless to say, it was difficult to blossom, let alone exist, in that sort of environment. It often felt like being stuck in prison. Life was just one constant, never-ending stream of torment that I could not escape. Depression and low self-esteem were just a small part of the equation though; underneath, simmering below the surface, was a growing and often intense rage. And sometimes, I just couldn't hold it back any longer.

For example, one night as my father began coaxing my sisters to verbally abuse me at the dinner table (again), I found myself pushed over the edge. Throwing my chair back, I jumped to my feet, screamed, clawed my nails down his back, and then fled the room. Running out the door and into the yard, I was followed by the sound of his laughter. It was like being in hell.

As a child, you want to be loved by your father. You want to be able to trust him. And you tend to keep hoping — despite what has happened in the past. This was especially true for me, given my hopeful, compassionate, and generous nature. Yet, every time I would gain confidence my father would strike it down (or somehow eliminate the chance before it could even happen). Every time I decided to trust him, I received cruelty instead. Every time I thought our relationship was improving, I would be proven wrong.

Unbelievably, I continued to hold onto hope even as a teenager; and then one day, something strange happened. All of a sudden, my father began to treat me differently. He was spending time with me and even showing kindness. He seemed to be making a real effort to develop a positive relationship. I was excited, happy, and hopeful; yet I was old enough, smart enough, and had gone through the cycle enough to notice the little voice of warning in the back of my mind. *This has to be too good to be true. There has to be more to this.*

I thought about what my gut was telling me but I didn't listen. Why? Well, after an entire childhood of wanting to be loved by my father, it seemed like my dreams were finally coming true. Oh, if only I had known the devastating and traumatic betrayal that was to come.

My father's intentions, as you've probably guessed, were quite different from what they seemed. Beneath the laughter, compliments and positive attention, lay his true motivation — which was to prey on his daughter, a young teenager starved for affection; a young woman who was just beginning to experience the awakening of her sense of sexuality. Yes, his intent was to betray the trust I had allowed and placed in him, by molesting me. The fact that he did this while my mother — his wife — was home, just went to show the absolute confidence he had in getting away with hurting me.

After the assault I knew that I needed to tell someone, so, quietly and nervously, I went upstairs to the main level of the house and sat down on the couch beside my mom. Shaking all over, I tried to open my mouth to speak, but before I could even get the words out she turned and spoke. "Did he touch you?" she asked directly.

My mom had guessed so quickly that I couldn't help but wonder: what signs had she seen? Why hadn't she divorced him before that, like she always talked about? I guess I'll never know, but she did end the marriage right there and then, and for that I am eternally grateful.

What happened was awful, but finally, after endless years of constant abuse my father was gone from my world. For the first time in my life, I thought freedom had finally arrived — not just in the form of my father's absence, but in the sudden opportunity for a real future. All around me were friends who were getting jobs, learning to drive, and talking about college; things that weren't a part of my world. 'Finally,' I thought to myself, 'maybe now I can experience something more than just chores and school!'

The reality, however, was bitterly disappointing. In the end, I merely moved from one type of prison to another. After so many years of my mother co-depending on my father, she — naturally — then transferred all of those unrealistic expectations onto me. Suddenly, I was expected to act as a spouse (in other words, a mature adult), as well as a parent to my sisters. Can you imagine what it was like trying to 'parent' and supervise two younger siblings — particularly when they had been taught to despise me? 'Disastrous' and 'futile' are probably the only words that really sum up that situation. And to add to it, whenever I called my mother at work for help (because my sisters were behaving so badly and wouldn't heed my instructions), she would get upset with *me*.

With everything going on, dealing with my mother's emotional dependence was probably the hardest part. Several times I found myself in shouting matches with her, trying to explain that my life needed to include more than just school and chores (you know, like spending time with friends and getting a job). But she rarely seemed to hear me. Instead, her response was to tell me about the things *she* needed, as if I was an adult who could share or shoulder the load. No matter how many times I tried to explain my perspective or feelings, she simply didn't hear me. At one point my aunt (who was my mother's sister and lived three hours away), tried communicating the same message on my behalf. Yet, my mother's response was always the same.

Tragically, not long afterwards, my aunt died suddenly from a brain aneurysm. At this stage, I had only *just* begun to pursue a closer relationship with her — to finally take a chance on someone who seemed to believe, and see, my situation. I had gotten as far as writing her a letter in an effort to begin building a stronger relationship; but tragically, she never received it. The letter was found in her mailbox after she died.

So, with that last, small light of hope suddenly extinguished, I started to spiral downward into an even deeper depression. From the depths of my darkness I watched my friends' lives continue to move forward; whereas for me, it felt like I was in quicksand. As my senior year approached, I thought to myself, 'After graduation, I am literally going to disappear. I will no longer exist; because my only reason for *being* is to take care of others and shoulder their load.'

It's fair to say that I probably would have seriously contemplated suicide had it not been, ironically, for my impending breakdown. You see, after 17 years of stuffing down every emotion and not having a confidant or outlet, things finally came to a head. I remember walking down the hall one morning, feeling completely normal, and then all of a sudden it was as if the floodgates that had been holding back my emotions for so many years burst wide open. It was so intense that I could feel every nerve in my body.

Just like my father's assault, I knew I had to tell someone about what was happening, and so I sought out my English teacher (who I trusted and who knew me well), telling her everything. As a result, the school reached out to my mother and she decided to take me to see a psychologist. Finally, there was an objective adult present to see my mother's behaviour for what it was, and to force her to start supporting me toward building my own life! It was thanks to this psychologist that I was able to get my drivers' license, a part-time job, and go on to be accepted into a local college.

For a while, things seemed hopeful again. I chose to move out and live on campus, and enrolled in a Creative Writing major. I continued working part-time, and for the first time in my life, I felt like things were heading in a positive direction.

Despite my newfound freedom, however, there were two things that still had a grip on me. One was a deep-seated need for love — something that had never been quenched growing up. The other was my mother, who was still a hugely negative influence in my life (as I worked at the same store she did and had to rely on her for transportation).

By the end of my first semester, I could feel myself sliding backwards into hopelessness and depression. It was clear that so long as my mother had access to my life, I would be subject to her dependencies and criticism. Deep down I knew with certainty that if I stayed where I was, I would end up in a very bad place. So, I made the decision to drop out of college and move in with my then-boyfriend and his family — even though they lived about two hours away. It was a necessary choice, but not one that led to great positive change.

Why? Because up until that point, my entire life had been about *surviving*. So, although I was finally and completely free from my childhood circumstances, I had extremely low self-esteem and even less self-confidence. I also hadn't been raised to make plans, have dreams, be ambitious, or create my own life. Plus, I was still desperate for love — not a great emotional place to enter a relationship from!

As a result, I spent the next few years aimlessly adrift. While I did manage to land a job that offered a livable wage — allowing me to move out and leave my deadbeat boyfriend — it should come as no surprise that I wasn't exactly succeeding at life. It was during this period of uncertainty that I met *Martin (who I later married).

While I had initially approached our relationship very cautiously, I now realise that I also saw him as a way out. So, when things began to go south with my employer, I quit my job, moved in with Martin, and married him in a simple courthouse ceremony a few months later.

What ensured was not a happy marriage, to say the least. Martin turned out to be an extremely manipulative and emotionally abusive man. He also made erratic, illogical, and irresponsible decisions on a routine basis — always expecting other people (myself included) to bear the consequences.

That said, it was also during this period of my life, that I began to blossom and change in amazing ways. (To be honest, I didn't plan to share this part of my journey when I first began writing my story; it's difficult to explain to many, but I also feel that my sudden transformation wouldn't make sense without sharing this.) The truth is, after a lifetime of deep trauma, I made a decision two years into my marriage to enter a relationship with Jesus. Through my faith, he became the first true cheerleader, protector, and father I'd ever had. He also began changing and healing me on the inside. As the years progressed, I stopped being immensely codependent on Martin, while standing up to his toxic and selfish behaviour. I began building real confidence and self-esteem, as well as healing from old wounds.

Eventually, nine years into our marriage, everything came to a head. Martin wanted to do something incredibly wrong, I said 'no' and stood my ground, and his response was to declare that we were divorcing. So here I was… 30 years old and starting my life over with only a few thousand dollars in the bank, whatever material possessions I could fit into my CR-V, and our dog 'Happy.' At this point I had a degree in web design but no full-time job, and so, with limited funds and nowhere else to go, I had zero choice but to move back in with my mother.

Once again, I was back in a toxic, unsupportive, and uncertain environment. But as depressing as this sounds, 2011 was the year that, at long last, I stopped simply 'surviving,' and finally began to truly *thrive*. It wasn't a simple process by any means, but over the next three years, I decided to make it my priority to keep moving forward and to not give up. I went from working in a thrift store — because I didn't believe I was talented enough to land a full-time web design job — to, well, getting a full-time design job! I also went from living with my mother (who eventually kicked me out), to two intermediate living situations (one with an awful roommate), to renting my current downtown apartment in Pittsburgh, PA — the city in which I now work. One of the most celebratory occasions during that time frame was the day I was able to finally — after three years — unclip the lids from all of my ugly grey storage tubs, and actually put *all* my belongings in their own space! It sounds silly, but there is so much joy in being able to actually organise your own stuff; to know you have a stable home.

Aside from all of this, there have been inward changes too. My confidence and self-esteem have continued to grow in leaps and bounds, along with the ability to stand up for myself. I've also learned a great deal about who I am and how I'm wired, as well as what I'm capable of and what I want out of life.

I've gone from a woman who didn't think she could get a basic 'nine to five' job, to a woman who did just that (and excelled at it). Slowly, but purposely, I'm now building my own business — one that I truly believe in and which I know will be successful.

I've gone from a young woman who never had dreams, and who saw her identity as only existing for others, to a woman who imagines herself travelling the globe, trying new things, and embracing the challenge of building her own life (all while helping others along the way).

As a young child and teen, life was about surviving. But now, it's so much more. I'm a woman who is finally living with purpose and *thriving*. A woman who is here to help others, and use her past to make a brighter future.

JENN MURRAY lives in Pittsburgh (PA) and is the founder of 'Relate Escape,' a business that plans events for entrepreneurs and corporate organisations. As an Event Strategist, Jenn is passionate about helping her clients create events that foster a sense of community and cultivate authentic connection — while also meeting their specific business goals. In her spare time, you'll find her walking her beloved ex-racing Greyhound 'Hobbs', or curling up with a historical fiction novel. Find out more about Jenn at relateescape.com.

Fai
(Thailand)

"I am no longer that little girl who dared not speak for fear of what others might say or think. No longer am I that angry young woman filled with pain and fear. Looking back, my past has helped me to grow into the strong woman I am today; someone who can see the pain inside others' hearts and understand the challenges that people face in life — and that is a special thing."

As a young girl, I grew up in a small part of Myanmar, not too far from the border of Tachileik. Like many families, we were very poor and life was hard for my mother. Having to look after three children on her own while her husband was imprisoned, was tough; but she did the best she could. Most of my days were spent attending a local kindergarten (as Myanmar was still very strict at this time with education), walking through the rich, red dirt that lined the village pathways, and picking vegetables by the canal or cutting wood. Sometimes my friends and I would play rubber jumping or hide-and-seek as the village dogs roamed around.

One day, however, my mother called me to her side and explained that she was no longer able to afford to look after me as well as my two sisters. So, at age six I was sent away to Thailand to live with my aunt and uncle. At the time I was excited, but as I soon came to discover, my aunt and uncle were not very loving people.

It was tough trying to settle into a new home and life where nothing was familiar — but school was another thing entirely. I was often accused of being a fool, and told I was 'stupid like an autistic child.' Every time I did something 'wrong' (which seemed to be all the time), my aunt would punish me. One of the ways she did so, was by grabbing me by the arm and marching us down to the village so that everyone could watch on as she told me what a bad person I was. "Why can't you be like your cousin?" she'd sneer. "Why do you have to be such a stupid girl? Can't you see how insulted everyone is by your presence? Ahh, you're just like your mother! No wonder you're such an awful and bad girl."

Standing there, as the whole village looked on, it was hard not to let her words into my heart. For many years afterwards, I dared not even speak most of the time. I just felt so worthless and stupid. All I wanted was love, for someone to care for me like the other children in our village. But there was no one to give me even a drop of kindness. I think that was when I made a decision to close myself off to everyone and everything.

Looking back, I was a very 'crabby' child, but in reality I was just in so much pain that I didn't know how to open up. I was so fearful of life, and it was hard to believe that anything good could ever come from my existence.

One early morning when I was about 11 years old, I climbed out of bed, got dressed, and began my daily ritual of cooking up a pot of rice. It was around 5 am, and the sun was not yet up, so I huddled closer to the warmth of the fireplace. As I lowered the pot onto the fire, my heart was suddenly overwhelmed by sadness. With my arms wrapped around my knees, I curled into a ball and let the tears trickle down to the earth flooring below. *'You'll never be anything,'* my head screamed. *'Your mother is far away, your father is dead, and what are you doing with your life? All you've done is prove that you're a useless, stupid child that no one cares for.'* As the tears flowed faster, I suddenly found myself thinking about a group of missionaries who had come through our village a few months earlier, and remembered how they had encouraged us to pray when we were sad or scared. To be honest, I wasn't very interested in their message when they came by (I only went to sit and listen because I wanted the free candy!); but at that moment, I felt so alone that I found myself asking God to help me. How, exactly, I didn't know? But I needed a way out of this awful, painful life — that much was true.

It was sometime shortly after this, that my aunt and uncle called me to them and said they needed to talk. *'Great, what have I done wrong this time,'* I thought to myself. "Fai, we have some news," began my aunt. "We know your mother cannot afford to continue supporting your study, but we've learned of a local dormitory who are looking for an orphan to raise. They want to give you a chance to study there."

I couldn't believe it. *'Is this actually happening?'* I wondered. Could someone actually care about me that much? I think this was the first time anyone had ever made me feel like I was special, or that I could be of value. Things like this just didn't happen to poor village girls — yet somehow, I had been thrown a miracle.

As I began to prepare my belongings and get ready to go to the orphanage, I felt the very first little spark within my soul, telling me that maybe, just maybe, I was not a useless, stupid child after all. It was only small, but it was enough.

My first day at the orphanage was filled with a mixture of nervousness and excitement. Having the chance to further my education — particularly as a young girl from a small village — was an incredible opportunity and not one that I took lightly. I was incredibly grateful, and having a sense of purpose and direction began to lessen the anger and pain I felt deep inside.

Yet, even so, life in the orphanage was not care-free. As I soon discovered, the orphanage provided us with just 10 baht per day for living expenses. The problem was, all our daily meals cost at least 12 baht. If I used my money to buy rice, I wouldn't have enough left over for my other daily needs — so most of the time I stuck to the cheap meals, like stir-fried Chayote leaf, bitter gourd, cabbage, or potato. Every day, I watched on as the other students devoured their rice and curry dishes or sipped on cold milk and tea, all while my stomach growled with hunger. Sometimes I would treat myself to one of the cheap two-baht snacks, but most of the time I saved my money. A lot of the time I went hungry. After all, unlike many of the other students, I had no family to support me.

Looking back, I know my friends would have helped if I'd asked — but I was too embarrassed and ashamed. It was hard enough trying to fit in at a new school, and the last thing I wanted was for my friends to look at me as 'the poor girl.' So instead, I would make excuses to sneak away and find an empty classroom to hide in. While everyone else was eating I would curl up on the floor, hugging myself into a ball and sleeping away the hunger.

If I thought going hungry was the worst that could happen though, I was in for a rude shock — because soon I was a young woman, and this meant further embarrassment. Now, as well as paying for food and studies, I also had to pay for sanitary napkins. Sometimes I would try to work really hard during the holidays, instead of resting, so that I could make enough money to cover my basic needs — but it never went far. The holidays were such a short period of time and the little money I made was always exhausted very quickly.

Even though life at the orphanage had many hardships, I tried to stay as focused as possible on my end goal — which was to make something of my life. When I graduated from grade nine, I realised that I had a strong desire to keep studying, but at that time, I wasn't sure how I would find someone to support me. It was a time of uncertainty, and at that moment I did fear that I would have to give up on my dreams. Deep down, however, I knew that life had looked after me so far, and so I decided to stay hopeful. *'Surely there has to be a way to make this work?'* I remember thinking. *'I've just got to stay positive.'* Soon afterwards, a friend of mine offered to introduce me to another dormitory that was also raising orphans. Realising that this was my chance to do something more with my life, I quickly applied, praying for a miracle.

A few weeks later, I found out that my submission had been accepted! Even more exciting, was that they would support all my expenses and provide 30 baht per meal! After so much struggle, and always feeling like an outsider, I could finally live like other kids my age. The relief was so sweet! For the first time in my life, I finally felt like I was thriving. I really loved my time at this dormitory, but eventually, the day came where it was time for me to leave. Going out into the 'real world' after finishing my studies was very difficult. Suddenly, there were no rules and no one to guide me. All of a sudden I was on my own. Even more difficult, however, was the prospect of finding work.

You see, getting a job can be very hard for young people in Thailand and paid opportunities don't come easily. So, while I was very excited to be offered a nursing internship straight after graduation, I also needed a part-time job that paid well enough for me to study and work at the same time. Around this time I was offered a job in a Mai Sai massage parlour; it was a job that I knew would help me get ahead financially, but at the same time I felt torn. I knew it was risky work. I'd heard many stories of girls being abused, harassed, or even trafficked, and I was nervous about what kind of environment it would be. I was also worried about what people would think of me. But at that moment, I realised I didn't really have a choice. I needed to make money and it was the only part-time job I could find.

For the most part, I was very lucky in the few months I worked at the parlour. Most people who came through were happy and friendly — but of course, not every customer was respectful. Some came for bad purposes and would seize any opportunity to grab us. The first time a man tried to touch me in a way I didn't like, I was filled with anger. I didn't want to end up like some of the girls in other local shops, and I knew I had to stand up for myself — or things might get much worse. On that occasion, I was lucky because the man did apologise and respect my wishes, but I knew that there was a risk involved with staying too long in the massage industry. At the end of the day, our safety depends almost entirely on the owners. If they don't care about their staff, they allow men to ask for certain things. If you're lucky, they make it clear that the shop is for relaxation purposes only. As I said, things were okay at the shop, but in my heart I still longed to go to university and study. I knew a miracle would have to happen for me to make my dreams come true, but once again I decided to stay positive, trusting and praying that the right opportunity would eventually come.

One day, a few months after I started at the shop, I was talking to a friend when suddenly she mentioned an organisation named Destiny Rescue. "You should go and see them," she suggested. "Maybe they can help you find a job or study a business course?" To be honest, it sounded too good to be true, and I really wasn't sure if I trusted them. I had heard bad stories of girls being tricked and hurt by traffickers, and I wasn't sure if they meant what they said about helping me.

However, once again I had that little feeling inside, urging me to take a chance. So, a few days later I went to visit some of the staff and see if what they were offering was true. That moment was the stepping stone to the rest of my life. It was the moment where the doors finally opened up, and I truly began to thrive. Not only were they providing me with a place to stay and a chance to study, but I was finally in a place where I felt like everyone cared and wanted to see me succeed. It felt like coming home.

When a program opened up for me to continue studying, I was so excited! To go from being a small village girl who no one believed in, to a young woman surrounded by people who want the best for you, is a feeling like no other. By stepping up for myself and taking this opportunity, I was able to get my Bachelor's degree in Business, and once I had this, it was amazing to see how quickly people's perceptions of me changed. Almost immediately my aunt and uncle's attitude toward me began to soften, and they finally seemed to recognise that I was, in fact, a smart young woman and that I had a future ahead of me.

Recently I started working as a receptionist at a hotel here in Thailand, and I feel so blessed to have the chance to spend every day learning new skills and working toward my future. I'm surrounded by great people and going to work finally gives me a sense of purpose and fulfilment. It's funny because in the past I never really allowed myself to dream of a future, but after so much struggle, and having come so far, I now know that anything is possible — if only we don't give up!

At present, my mother still lives in Myanmar and I miss her a lot. While I'm still young though, I'm determined to do everything I can to make the most of the opportunities I've been given so that I can give back to my family. One day I hope to be able to fulfil my dream of buying a house and land so that my mother can finally be reunited with my sisters and I here in Thailand.

While writing my story, I thought of all the other children out there who have gone through difficult childhoods like mine. All the children who are alone, who feel lost, or who go to bed hungry. I think of the children who, like me, felt stupid and useless. When Jas asked me to share my story in this book, she asked me what I'd like to say to other children who have gone through trauma or abuse, and after some thought, this is what I want to share: No matter how unfairly life has treated you, you are valuable. No matter how many burdens you carry alone, you are valuable. And even when it feels like no one else could understand how you are feeling, you are still valuable. Only now can I say this, after having walked this road myself. Looking back, my past has helped me to grow into the woman I am today; someone who can see the pain inside others' hearts and understand the challenges that people face in life — and that is a special thing.

I am no longer that little girl who dared not speak for fear of what others might say or think. No longer am I that angry young woman filled with pain and fear. Today, I am a strong woman with a heart that can easily forgive others, and courage to dream big and explore the future. I am proud of who I am and how far I've come.

FAI lives in Thailand and is a graduate of Destiny Rescue's Prevention Education program. To find out more about Destiny Rescue and their work in rescuing child trafficking victims, and providing education pathways to vulnerable or at-risk young people, visit destinyrescue.org.

REASONS TO LIVE...
Surviving & Thriving with Bipolar Disorder

A note from Jas Rawlinson

"OMG, he was acting so bipolar."

Okay, let's be honest. Chances are, you've probably heard someone use this kind of comment from time to time… Maybe it was even you? If so, don't be too hard on yourself — even I've been guilty of making throw-away remarks like this in the past. I know I didn't mean any offence at the time, but the truth is, I was blissfully ignorant about what it's truly like to battle this disorder every day of your life.

The thing is, when we talk about mental health, most people tend to think primarily of depression and anxiety. However, of the many other types of mental illness that people can experience, I would argue that bipolar disorder tends to receive far less empathy or understanding than 'mainstream' disorders. In fact, prior to high-profile people like Kevin Hines (international suicide prevention speaker and award-winning documentary filmmaker) rising to global recognition and sharing the truth of what it's like to live with bipolar, I think many of us had no idea just how much of a daily battle it is to keep on top of the highs and lows.

What has stood out to me the most while working with both Jason and Ashlee (whose stories you're about to read), is how long it took the two of them to receive an accurate diagnosis, as well as to find the right mix of prescription medications and self-care strategies. Both of these brave individuals have walked very different journeys, yet also experienced many of the same feelings and thoughts. Likewise, both have had to dig deep and find a way out of the darkness.

With that said, I'd like to introduce you to my two 'Bipolar Warrior Writers,' Jason and Ashlee. As an added bonus, when you get to the end of this section you'll also find an exclusive interview feature between myself and Kevin Hines.

Jason Rantall
Trafalgar, VIC (Australia)

Image credit: SuperSport Images

"If I could go back now and speak any words of wisdom to myself, I would tell the little boy with dreams to keep dreaming; I would tell him to never give up and to keep fighting. I'd say, 'Mate, as hard as it gets, keep fighting. Life is going to be tough, but everything will be okay. Believe in you and never lose sight of what you want, who you are, and what you dream.'"

I was only nine years of age when my mum found me with my head in the toilet, trying to drown myself. I have lived with brain pain and thoughts of suicide for as long as I can remember. An overwhelming hatred and dislike for myself, I guess you could call it.

Growing up, I knew very strongly that my thoughts and emotions were not normal. From irrational outbursts of emotion (I'd often swing like a pendulum between manic excitement and absolute despair) to 'feeling' and 'believing' that earwigs were eating my brains, these were just everyday 'norms' for me. It was very clear that that my thoughts and feelings were more than just the vivid imagination of a little boy; yet no one could find an answer.

Doctor, after doctor, after doctor…I saw so many medical professionals during my childhood and each one had a different opinion: *"It's your family environment;" "He's just an attention seeker;" "It's puberty."* At no point did they listen to my cry for help or entertain the thought of a young child having a mental illness. Even I, as a little boy, knew it had to be more than just my surroundings. It was something deep, something that was part of my genetic makeup and who I was. But no one listened. In fact, as I recently discovered, they used to tell Mum to stop wasting their time by bringing me in so often! I can't imagine how tough it was for her, dealing with all of this as a young mother. She was only 17 when she gave birth to me, and my little brother Glenn was born barely two years later. Being a teenage mum to two little boys — one of whom had something peculiar going on with his behaviour and thoughts — and then becoming a single parent at just 19, would be a lot for anyone to deal with.

These ups and downs were — unfortunately — a pattern that continued for much of my childhood. A short time later mum met someone new, who she married and then went on to have another baby with (my little sister); but soon afterwards their relationship broke down. So now my young mum had three little people to care and provide for!

I really feel for mum and what those years must have been like. I've always been super protective of her, and despite our hardships I know that she did the best she could for us kids. Still, being without a strong father figure for most of your childhood is tough for a young boy, and so from a very young age, I took it upon myself to be the father-figure for my brother and sister. I knew it was important — even though I was only six years old. Cooking, cleaning, babysitting; it was all normal to me. I didn't mind the hard work though. To be honest, it was a role I really wanted to fulfil.

I was lucky to have a good relationship with my step-dad 'Sticks' (as we called him), and to this day I still do, but the man who made the biggest difference in my life was my pop. He taught me how to embrace being a young imaginative boy, and as a grown man I still use his teachings today. With Nan tucking me into the big comfy sheets of their flannelette bed, her voice softly reading stories of 'The Gingerbread Man', and Pop mucking around making me laugh, I felt a sense of security that I desperately needed as a little boy. Both of them played a huge part in making me who I am today, and I miss them both dearly.

Although I didn't have a 'traditional family dynamic' (in the sense), the one thing that did play a role in my downfall was alcohol. Most dark places I've ever found myself in — many reckless decisions, relationship breakdowns, or acts of violence — have been influenced by this addiction; an addiction that started before I had even turned 15.

For me, alcohol was like a magic potion. With every sip, there was immediate and overwhelming relief. Every crazy thought seemed to disappear. It was unbelievable! So it was here, as a young teen, that my love for what alcohol could do for me was born. Of course, with this newfound 'love' came a whole truckload of other troubles; issues that, until a year ago, almost robbed me of my life many times over.

During my later teenage years, I spent a lot of time struggling to make sense of what was going on inside my mind. Trying to fit in and hide my troubling thoughts, feelings, and emotions was probably the most difficult part of high school — and of course, tipping alcohol on this just made everything worse. By the time I was 16 or so, I just couldn't take it anymore, and after a night of heavy drinking I decided to curl up on the cold asphalt of a busy side street in my friend's housing estate. I guess I was just hoping a car would take me out and end the pain for me. Thankfully, my friend found me, dragged me to my feet, and took me home.

My grades at school were good and my work was of a high standard up until I started drinking too much. I passed Year 11, but from there started to struggle. Year 12 was an absolute disaster. On one night, I stayed up drinking until 2 am the day before a major exam. I just couldn't get it together. During this time, I also had a major falling out with Mum (which was extremely painful for me), and things between her and my step-dad ended.

As the days wore on, my world began to spin further out of control. Soon, life became little more than 'treading water.' And so it was that the following years passed by in a haze of alcoholism, countless stupid decisions, and recklessness (including a head-on with a semi-trailer). My 'need' for alcohol was so severe that I'd often burn through 20 cans of alcohol on a Friday, go to sleep at 4 am, smash another 12-20 cans on Saturday (depending on how sick I felt), and then finish the weekend with a further 12 drinks. Weekdays weren't much better. Two six-packs and 40-50 smokes per day were the norm for me. Unbelievably, I almost never missed a day of work.

One night out on the town, I happened to meet a young woman named Tanya. At the time, she had an 18-month-old daughter named Erryn, and as our relationship grew more serious, we added to our family with a little girl of our own. I was still a mess, but hoping desperately for a better future.

Interestingly, the year Jaimee was born turned out to be a major turning point in my life, because this was the moment where

I finally received an answer to what was going on inside my head. After 24 years! By this stage, Tanya had been trying for around three years to get me the help I needed. Drinking and smoking cigarettes was all I cared about, and unsurprisingly, our relationship had turned toxic — particularly given that my depression and mania were at an all-time high. Somehow, she got me to agree to see a doctor, and this was when I finally discovered the truth: I had obsessive compulsive disorder and type one bipolar disorder. The relief I felt was incredible! *'Finally, a legitimate medical explanation for my emotions, actions, and thoughts,'* my mind mused. With the doctor's instructions to take medication and cut back on alcohol, I was genuinely excited about the prospect of living a 'normal' life. So, off I went, skipping and optimistic about how different life was going to be.

For a while there I did change my ways, and life looked pretty good. I was medicated, eating healthily, drinking less, and getting fit — all positive things. I'd also started buying and renovating multiple properties with my mate Doc. Financially I was hitting good strides, and all the dreams I'd had as a little boy of wealth and success were starting to become a reality. "Man, look at Jason, he's really got his shit together," people would say.

What the world couldn't see, was that it was all a facade…

Behind the renovations, beautiful home, and rental properties, was a man who was unravelling from the inside. Why? Well, once again, alcohol had sweet-talked its way into my daily routine. It started slowly, but before I knew it, I had once again become its slave. My relationship was falling apart, my brain was aching, and everything felt like a mess. Looking in the mirror became a nightmare. *'You're a burden,'* screamed my reflection. *'Your children are better off without you. You're shit at your job. You're too much hard work.'* The level of self-hatred I had was unbelievable, but the only thing worse were the suicidal thoughts. They were constant. So, I did what I always did; I chose to drink the pain away. But before long, the alcohol no longer gave me the excitement and relief it once did, so I made the decision to 'end it'; to end my pain and the pain I was causing those I loved.

Sitting in that dark place, fighting every natural instinct inside of you to live — to keep breathing at all costs — is a fight I don't wish on anyone. Many fail to understand just how much of a battle it is. It's not just a random thought. It's not just a down day. It's a literal mental battle; a war where you are *fighting* to live. What I didn't realise at the time though, was that I wasn't just making the choice to die; I was also choosing to end any opportunity to have the life I dreamt of as a child. I was choosing to end my chance at happiness and the possibility of one day positively impacting the world — in any way.

Over the next few years I made several attempts on my life, including an attempted hanging (which resulted in the tree branch breaking, smacking me on the head, and leaving me flat on my ass — just so you know). I am grateful that I was able to walk away from that with just a concussion and a broken rope. There were of course many other things I tried, although I don't need to go into detail. What is important, is to make it clear that whatever I tried, none of it was necessary. Yes, I wanted the pain to end — but killing myself wasn't the solution.

The thing is, when there is no will to live, there is very little fear (if any) – and when it came to recklessness, I was a pro. One time I even started a fight with a bikie leader and his gang! (Okay, so it wasn't much of a fight — he hit me hard and I hit the deck.) Let's just say, I was lucky that my mate Dutchy and some of the security guards got me out of there before those blokes ended me!

Throughout these years there were many occasions where I spent time recovering in hospital or locked up in psych wards. It was an awful time and I'm very grateful for the support I had from family and friends during these stays, in particular, the love shown by my beautiful friend Juan. He visited me every single day during one of my longest stays and really kept my spirits up. My mate Doc (who I had spent years renovating properties with) was also a huge support, and 20 years later, he still hasn't given up on me! When you're in such a dark place, knowing that there's someone who cares enough to give so much of their time to you, means more than many could ever comprehend.

In a way, I guess those psychiatric stays kept me away from harm for a period of time, but I still had a long way to go and a lot of pain to work through. Over the next few years I lost my family unit as well as my house, and also racked up massive credit card debt (which I'm still paying off today). I drank, partied, drank, spent money I didn't have, and partied some more. By now, the life I dreamt of as a little boy had all but vanished and I felt powerless to do anything. I felt like I'd failed at being an adult. *'Just let me go, please,'* begged my soul. *'I can't do life anymore, please stop this pain. Please make it end.'* Little did I know, however, that life was about to throw me a light; a beacon in the darkness.

One hopeless night while getting ready to drink myself into oblivion at a mate's house, I met a woman named Kerry; the woman who would become my now wife and the love of my life. To be honest, I still have no idea what she saw in me that night. You can probably imagine what I looked like at this stage of my life: overweight, angry, drunk. I mean, what a catch!

Anyway, for one reason or another we hit it off straight away, and within a few months we had moved in together. We combined our debts (loads of them), and children (loads of them too!), and set out on our new life together. I still joke that if only my beautiful wife knew what she was in for, she probably wouldn't have entered into this relationship! (But I'm so glad you did babe.)

Instantly, Kerry set about learning everything she could about my illness and how to support me. Even as I write this, nine years on from when we met, she is currently studying a Certificate IV in Alcohol and Drugs, as well as a Diploma in Mental Health.

It hurts me to think of how much pain I must have caused her throughout my journey to wellness, but for reasons I will never know, she has never run away from any of our challenges. Kerry has been my rock, my saviour, my love, and my best friend; both in sickness and in health.

Since meeting Kerry, I've discovered so much about myself and my life passions. Running has become a huge part of my physical and mental recovery, but with this newfound love, I've also learned about the importance of 'moderation.' For a long time, exercise was just another way of punishing myself, because I was running to the point of exhaustion in an attempt to keep away the brain pain. "See ya Forrest Gump!" my wife would call, as I headed out the door each day. It was funny, but also true — I was running myself into the ground.

It was strange. I'd changed so many aspects of my life, yet unbelievably, the pain felt worse than ever. The best thing I did during this time, was to reach out on a mental health Facebook group that I had just recently created, and to admit that I wasn't well. I felt so vulnerable sharing about my life, but to my relief The Universe answered. That day, a beautiful man named David Camilleri from Strength of Mind Body reached out and offered a hand.

The very next day I drove over an hour to see Dave. 100%, that meeting changed my life. It transformed me into who I am today.

Of course, there were lots of things I had to address — starting with my unhealthy lifestyle choices. The first thing I did was to switch to a ketogenic diet and cut down on time spent running (as the constant exhaustion wasn't helping my depression). But those were just small changes. Over the next few months, Dave motivated me to search deeply and find who I was; to find the 'real Jason' and believe that I had the power to change my story and rewrite the rules for my life. With Dave's support, I began to grow — month by month, and step by step. For the first time in 45 years my life had purpose.

Today, I'm able to live free from medication and keep myself well by following my '7 Pillars of Health': Gratitude, meditation, mindfulness, communication, reflection, healthy diet, and exercise. I find that gratitude, in particular, plays a huge role in my ability to stay well. In theory it's such a simple tool, but after reading 'The Magic' by Rhonda Byrne, I came to understand more fully just how powerful it is. There are many amazing books out there, but this one had a massive impact on me in ways I never anticipated, and many of the exercises listed in the book are things I still do today (like journaling). Since implementing these tips and strategies, I've been able to quit smoking (Jan 30th, 2017), get into regular exercise, and get completely sober (July 14th, 2018). All I can say is: thank you Rhonda!

For a long time I didn't believe it, but the truth is, I really do have so much to live for, and so many who care for me. Together, Kerry and I have three little ones of our own (or four, if you include our little guy Jack, who we unfortunately lost at 21 weeks pregnancy), and Kerry has two older daughters, who are 20 and 12. When you add in my two older daughters Jaimee and Erryn, we're one big, blended, vibrant family! I've also been able to reconnect with my biological father, Graham, and I'm still close to my mum. After everything she went through to provide for us kids growing up, I'm so thankful that she's gone on to find a loving and supportive partner. She and Nat have been together for over 25 years now, and I see him as part of our family.

By opening up about my journey, I've also come to meet many amazing people who've been where I am and found a way out, and I now have a whole new tribe of positive people and advocates who really help me stay on track — whether that be my church family or my fellow mental health advocates. These days I leap out of bed in the mornings, and I'm truly excited about what the day will bring. In the last year I've become qualified as a gym instructor, have achieved my Certificate III, and am currently studying my Certificate IV in

Personal Training and Fitness. Every month I run a monthly mental health community event, as well as my 'Brainercise' meetups, which are all about getting locals together to do some light group exercise, enjoy the sunshine, and have a coffee and a chat. In my opinion, bringing community together face to face is vital, and I believe exercise is a great way to do so.

The last 12 months has already thrown plenty of challenges my way, but now I feel stronger and more able to face them. It's funny, because change was something I used to hate; change challenged me. Now I look for challenges to change me. I know that if I want better, I have to do better. If I do today what I did yesterday, and do nothing but repeat this pattern, I'll be in the same place I've always been.

If I could go back now and speak any words of wisdom to myself, I would tell the little boy with dreams to keep dreaming; I would tell him to never give up and to keep fighting. I'd say, 'Mate, as hard as it gets, keep fighting. Life is going to be tough, but everything will be okay. Believe in you and never lose sight of what you want, who you are, and what you dream. Do what makes you smile from the inside; that really deep smile — because that is where the directions to your purpose lie.'

Happiness is something we all search for, but it's only when you accept and understand who you were made to be, and who you truly are, that you'll find it. It's no coincidence that when I found my purpose, I found myself. Only then was the brain pain, the beast that is mental illness and alcoholism, defeated.

Find your reason; your why; your purpose. Live the life you desire and deserve.

Believe, Do, Achieve.

JASON RANTALL lives in Victoria with his wife and family. Together, he and Kerry are the founders of 'Bettermentall.' Passionate about using health and fitness to empower others to live their best lives, he can often be found running marathons, or hosting monthly community meet ups and 'Brainercise' sessions in his town of Trafalgar. You can join their community online via @Bettermentall_Together (IG) or Bettermentall (FB).

Ashlee Reid
Weipa, QLD (Australia)

"Whenever I struggle with low moments, I feel scared that what happened to me after having Mckenna is going to happen again. But I'm working on that fear, and I know I'll get through it. Something that I hold firmly to, however, is this: I have bipolar, but I am not bipolar. These days, when people see this big old happy smile on my face, it's no longer painted on for show — now it's for real. And when the smile turns to turmoil and tears, I'm no longer afraid to ask for help."

Just a small-town girl getting through life the best way she knew how — that's pretty much the best way to sum up my life. Growing up in the far north Queensland town of Mareeba, nothing exciting ever really happened — but I was okay with that.

As a child, I think I always knew my head was a little different. I was pretty eccentric in the way I dressed, and often loved being the life of the party. At the same time, though, I could hide away for days on end, just reading or sleeping. This usually happened when something went wrong, or when a situation felt out of my control. For the most part my family never really worried, but I do remember a time where my dad became a little concerned by my excessive sleeping and tried to find out what was going on. Back then, I just shrugged it off with my biggest, brightest smile, assuring him that I was fine and it was no big deal.

Given that I grew up in a small town in the 1990s, there was no awareness of mental health, so at the time, there was really nothing to give me any insight into what was behind my 'eccentric' personality. As they say though, hindsight is a wonderful thing. It's only now that I can see how bad things really were — like all the times I worried myself into such a state of panic about my school work, that I'd end up vomiting in the bathrooms.

From those early years of high school, purging became my main coping mechanism. Not only was I vomiting from stress, but I was also making myself sick just to try and be like the girls around me. It's strange, because I had such a wonderful group of friends at the time but I never shared with anyone what was going on in my head.

Looking back, I often wonder, *'Why didn't I seek help?'* Logically I know that I should have. At the time though, I just had no idea who to tell. I was also scared. *'What if they think I'm crazy? What if I speak out and they tell me I'm just seeking attention?'* Those little voices always ended up winning out.

As difficult as it was to deal with these feelings on my own, I'm thankful that I not only had a wonderful and loving family, but also a beautiful group of friends — most of whom I still keep in contact with today. My school friends may not have realised just how much I was struggling, but their support, laughter and mischief definitely kept me going. I think that's one of the most beautiful things about growing up in a small town — you make a lot of wonderful lifelong friends who love you no matter what, and quite often you end up knowing their entire family! Those years were tough, but those friendships definitely helped me get through.

After finishing school, I went on to pick up a job as a dental assistant. It was never something I was passionate about, but the opportunity basically fell into my lap and it was a good job. However, shortly afterwards, our family was rocked by an awful tragedy and it hit us all pretty hard. Without going into detail, one of our family lost a child, and it was truly an awful time. To get through it, I think I just tried to ignore how much my heart was aching. During this time my sister Renee (who had always been my lifeline in troubled times) decided to move to a different state. Feeling a little lost, I decided to make the move 50 minutes away from home to the tropical North Queensland city of Cairns.

Life in Cairns, I have to say, definitely wasn't the best. Maybe it's because this was the period where I truly noticed how bad my anxiety was (although I can't honestly say I really knew what anxiety was at this point). My solution? To party it all away.

Party, party, party — that was my motto; and when I wasn't partying, I was either sleeping or constantly on the go with my work. As part of that job I did a lot of flying, and before too long I'd grown used to being on a plane every other week. But then something strange happened. One day, three years into my job, I experienced a panic attack. It was so sudden and severe that the staff had to remove me from the plane.

By now I knew that things in my life were not going well and that I needed to make changes to my lifestyle, so when I was presented with an opportunity to transfer to a position in Weipa, I took it. Thinking it was going to be a magic fix for my mental health, I threw myself into work, naively believing everything would soon fall into place. I was wrong. As a town, Weipa is very cliquey and for a long time I struggled to make friends. Soon, that ugly little voice from my teenage years crept back into my head... *'If you were skinny, you'd make friends more easily, Ash. Just lose some weight and you'll start fitting in.'* Once again I turned to bulimia, thinking it would 'fix' everything. Oh how wrong I was.

That first year was very lonely, but after almost 12 months things began to change when a receptionist from my work invited me on a girls' trip. What a weekend! Finally I was making friends — and even better, the trip ended up being the place where I would meet my future husband!

For the first time in forever, things were great. Alex made me happier than I'd ever been and I was travelling pretty well with my emotional health. However, a few years into our relationship we had a quad bike accident, and suddenly, all the anxiety from my younger years came hurtling back. I started making excuses not to go anywhere that involved 4-wheel driving (which is pretty much all you do in Weipa). Then I started isolating myself more and more. You'd think this would be the red flag I needed to reach out for help. But once again, I shrugged it off with a bright, happy smile and a flash of laughter. In some ways it's a decision I still regret to this day, because shortly afterwards I discovered I was pregnant — and this was where the real rollercoaster began.

Don't get me wrong, I was elated to be having a baby! Sick — oh so sick — but excited all the same. We did all the normal things that couples do; setting up the nursery, buying all the best baby stuff. There was nothing wrong with any of this but I think I had an unrealistic view of what motherhood was really like. *'I'll breeze through it,'* I thought naively. *'I mean, I've got eight nieces and nephews; I've been around plenty of babies. How much more prep do I need?'*

Of course, expectation and reality ended up being two very different things.

Giving birth was one of the most terrifying experiences of my life. Not only did I need to be induced, but I also fell ill with a vomiting bug at the same time! *'This is not my birth plan,'* I remember thinking. I mean, I didn't have a specific plan per se, but in my head I just expected to ace it — you know, no drugs; no one by my side except Alex. How wrong I was! Not even halfway through labour, I was begging him to call Mum. I was so glad I did. Even though she couldn't make things better, she talked me through every awful moment and kept reassuring me that I would be okay.

When Mckenna finally arrived, it truly was the most magical moment. I loved her so fiercely; more than I had ever expected to. It was pretty special to see both Mum and Alex beaming with excitement and just as eager to introduce Mckenna to the world. Let me tell you, nothing can prepare you for that sort of love, and to be honest, I think it's what got me through the next year. A year that would be hell on earth.

From the moment Mckenna was born, there was no chance to rest. I'd torn so badly after birth that I'd lost almost half my blood capacity and had to be rushed to a bigger hospital. I thought that was going to be my biggest hurdle, but again, life had other surprises in store for me.

The next week was like a whirlwind and unfortunately my memory of that time is still a little foggy (actually the next two years are a little foggy!). But essentially, I was handed motherhood, postnatal psychosis, and type one bipolar disorder all in the same deck of cards!

Everything began to unravel the night I came home from the hospital. Mckenna wouldn't sleep, and I was struggling to keep up enough milk for her. All night long I panicked; I just had no idea what to do. The worst thing was, every time I put my head on the pillow and tried to drift off, I would startle awake — it was like that weird 'falling' sensation you get when you're on the verge of sleep. I just couldn't get a single minute of rest and by the next day I was an absolute mess. I called the lactation consultant at the hospital and asked her to come around to our house, hoping there was something she could do. "Try not to worry too much, it's probably just a case of 'baby blues,'" she stated, before suggesting that I come back to the hospital for a night. She didn't seem too worried, but I decided to go back in anyway.

As soon as I got back to the hospital I began to fade fast. Within the first few days I'd dropped around 15kg, and the doctors were in a panic, desperately trying to find out what was going on. Eventually, a blood and iron transfusion were ordered, and as my physical health began to recover, I believed that my exhaustion, anxiety, and panic would also lift.

Immediately after the transfusion I told Alex I wanted to go outside, so he grabbed a wheelchair, popped Mckenna in my arms, and started pushing us down the hall. With tears in my eyes I looked down at her, and just felt…Well, all I know is I didn't want to hold her. (But there was no way I could say that out loud, right?!) As we headed down the corridor toward the outside courtyard, I noticed the familiar faces of my parents walking toward us. Mum — being the ever-doting nanna — immediately scooped Mckenna up for a cuddle. The moment she was out of my arms I was flooded with relief. That was the moment I realised something was very, very wrong.

'How on earth am I going to survive this?' I thought.

"Are you okay Ash? Something just doesn't feel right." Avoiding my older sister's gaze, I struggled to answer. I felt like the worst mother in the world, but as hard as it was, I knew I had to get everything off my chest. With a lump in my throat I turned toward Melissa's worried face and let the words rush out. "I don't know, I love her so much, I know I do, but when I see you and Mum holding Mckenna I have this overwhelming urge to leave and watch on from a distance," I admitted. "I feel like you guys will look after her better than I ever could. You'll be the parents she needs." As the words left my lips, relief flooded through my system. For the first time in my life I had chosen to be honest instead of hiding behind a smile. (I later discovered that Melissa made this decision to confront me after a family meeting with my parents and my sister Shannon; being the eldest, I think they thought she would be the best one to talk to me).

Immediately I made an appointment with my GP, and to my relief, was handed a prescription for antidepressants the very next day. *'Maybe now everything will be okay,'* I pondered. Relief, however, was short lived. As my GP explained, the medication would take more than a month to begin working… And I knew I couldn't wait that long.

'Six weeks?' I asked, terror coursing through my brain. *How on earth am I going to survive this feeling for the next month and a half?* Honestly, never have I been so petrified for my own safety.

I don't think I even lasted one night at home before I cracked. Everything within me was screaming for an end to the mental pain; for the 24/7 anxiety and fear to stop. And I knew right then and there, that if I didn't say something, I wouldn't survive. It took all the strength I had to turn to my husband and see his face crumple as I told him very clearly: "please take me back to the hospital, or I'm going to kill myself."

Immediately, Alex helped pack a bag and we walked to the car. I still remember Mum and Renee following us out the front door, begging me to stay. "Please don't go back to the hospital Ash, we can help you here. We'll get through this." It was like a knife to my heart. All throughout my life my family have been there for me, and I know how desperately they wanted to make things better, but at that point no one knew just how bad things were inside my head. I hope they now know how much I truly wished they could have fixed me that day. But not for one second do I regret my decision.

So back to the hospital I went. Being there alone without Mckenna truly made me feel like the worst mum in the world. After a few nights I was told that she needed to be brought in to see me, and by this stage, you'd probably think I would have been relieved — but once again I fell apart. That was the night two nurses found me rocking in the corner, inconsolable and filled with turmoil. Desperately, they willed me to go back to bed. *'Please help me!'* I wanted to scream. It felt like a freight-train was rattling through my head.

The next morning, I was sent for a psychiatric evaluation. This was my chance to finally get help — yet I didn't. *'Don't be silly Ash, they'll lock you up and throw away the key if you tell them about the voices!'* my mind taunted. *'Even worse, they'll take Mckenna away.'* Irrational as it may sound, this was a very real fear. If I'm completely honest, it's a fear that has continued to torture me up until very recently.

It was only through the help of medication and talk therapy that I was able to get through that time. Thankfully, I rebounded very quickly and also began to bond with Mckenna — even more so than most people believed possible. In fact, I was on top of the world! (Perhaps a little too much, if you get where this is going). As you can probably guess, however, there's an inevitable crash that often happens after experiencing postnatal psychosis. And oh my, do you crash!

The depression that enveloped me at this point was so deep that my parents had to drive up to Weipa to help. It was like nothing I'd ever been through. Nothing worked; nothing helped. Things were so bad I was almost catatonic. This was definitely *not* postnatal depression. It was so much more than 'baby blues.'

As a last resort, my doctor suggested electroconvulsive therapy — all 12 rounds. Living in a remote location like Weipa meant that there was no support like this in our town, so we had to travel to wherever that help was. Instantly we got busy packing, and within a few hours the three of us were in the car and on our way. With my parents following in tandem, we drove all night to reach the nearest hospital that could help — a massive 800kms away.

Immediately I was admitted to hospital as an inpatient (a decision that probably saved my life at that point). However, I think the major turning point came after Alex went back to Weipa for work, because it meant moving back in with my parents and getting real with myself. For some reason, no matter how much support I had from my family, all I wanted to do was push them away (something I still, to this day, struggle to forgive myself for). It took my eldest sister Melissa and her fierce 'take no crap' approach to pull me into line, and oh man, did I need it! At the time I was so angry at her for holding me accountable, but I'm so grateful she did. I was searching for some kind of quick fix, but when it comes to mental health there just isn't one. No magic pill; nothing. You have to fight and work for it daily. This is something I've been doing ever since.

While the highs and lows continued for around two years, eventually my doctors felt comfortable enough to confirm a diagnosis — type one bipolar disorder. Ironically, it came on the 13th of September 2018, the day we celebrate *R U OK? Day*.

How did I feel about being diagnosed? I don't really know. In some ways it was a relief, and I'm so grateful to be a lot more stable in my emotional and mental health. Even so, there's no magic fix, and whenever I struggle with low moments, I do often feel scared that what happened to me after having Mckenna is going to happen again. But I'm working on that fear, and I know I'll get through it. I also know that from time to time I may appear to be a lazy person with no drive, but when you have a brain as active as mine, sometimes getting out of bed uses all the energy you can muster for that day — and anything else you achieve is just a bonus.

I think a common theme that shows throughout my story is that, for so long, I was always too afraid to seek help. That is why I'm so passionate about sharing stories and ideas on how to help ourselves and each other. For me, self-care is about writing, sticking to routine, reading lots, and hugging my daughter and her daddy so damn tight each and every day that I hear them squeal with delight.

They say it takes a village to raise a child, and that's a phrase that always rings loudly in my mind. I'll never forget the love and kindness of my friends who came and visited me while in hospital, many of whom were also my lifeline during our school years. They reminded me of all the wonderful things I had to live for. So, to my whole village — Mum, Dad, Alex, my sisters, extended family, in-laws, my friends, and my Weipa 'family' — you have all helped save my life. Together, you have helped me become the best mum I could be, and to find the pot of gold at the end of the rainbow. To my husband: I never give you enough credit, but I want to say that you have definitely delivered on your promise to love me through sickness and in health — and with your whole heart! People like you are so hard to find; you're the kind of person who sees the good in everyone and where hate is such a foreign concept. But the thing I'm most grateful for is how you love me every day no questions asked. With a role model like you I can't wait to see how wonderful Mckenna's life is going to be.

And finally, to my daughter, I can't think of any better way to end this chapter than with a poem. This one's for you my love.

An open letter to my baby girl: Mckenna Jade

I've made it no secret we didn't get off to the best start
When I had you baby girl, I nearly fell apart
You see my silly brain it played some tricks on me
It almost made me certain motherhood wasn't meant to be
I was told that we may have no bond and I may feel no connection
But two years on my pretty girl, I look at you and can see my reflection
I've held so much guilt deep inside about how our first few weeks went
It's a gruelling guilt I feel all the time and it often doesn't relent
I thought motherhood was going to be the end of me but oh how I was wrong
Mckenna you're such a beautiful girl both amazing and so strong
As long as I have you my baby girl, I'll keep fighting this crazy fight
Because one day when I was looking down the tunnel, I found you — my shining little light.

ASHLEE REID lives in the remote QLD town of Weipa (Australia) and enjoys spending time with family, reading, and exploring nature on their ATV Buggy. Passionate about shining a light on postpartum psychosis, she often shares her story through social media with friends, family, and those looking to understand more about bipolar disorder.

Special Feature: 3 Questions with Kevin Hines

Golden Gate Bridge Suicide Survivor, International Storyteller & Award-Winning Documentary Filmmaker

For someone who spends almost every day of the year touring the world and sharing his wellness tips with millions of people, you'd probably be forgiven for thinking that Kevin Hines would be the first to notice when his mental health is declining. And yet, the last year has been one of his most challenging. There were secrets; secrets that even those closest to him did not know for quite some time. And those secrets led Kevin to spiral so deeply into mania, that at times, he couldn't even recognise his loved ones.

"I remember I'd turn to my wife some days and ask, 'Why are you in my bed?'" he shared with me, his eyes tinged with sadness. "She would show me photos of my father, and I'd just look at them blankly and say, 'I don't know that man.' One day I called my best friend, and he couldn't even understand me. He thought it was a crank call.

It's not something Kevin has spoken about in much detail up until now, and as he shared in our interview, he's still recovering from the damage done to his brain throughout that period of time in 2018.

Brave, doesn't even come close to describing many of the things Kevin opened up to me about. I mean, just try to imagine what it must be like for someone to reveal these truths to their loved ones — let alone the millions of people who look up to you? It's no small feat, that's for sure. But if you know anything about Kevin, authenticity and vulnerability are what he breathes, and he wouldn't be the man — or influential figure — he is, if he didn't speak honestly about his struggles.

It is my hope that as you read through Kevin's words below, you'll be inspired to know deep within your core that no matter what you are going through, you are not alone. Even those who appear strongest, fall down at times, and even more importantly, it's not our traumas or failures that define us — it's what we do with our pain and struggle that determines who we are.

Below, are a few highlights from our interview that we'd like to share with you, and although we speak primarily about what it's like to live with bipolar disorder, I believe that everyone can gain something from Kevin's words.

JR: In 2018 you were admitted to hospital after experiencing severe bouts of mania. Can you share a bit about this time and how your physical health contributed to your breakdown?

KH: I think what's most crucial for people to understand, is that I'm a guy who is religious about taking medication every day and sticking to a routine. I'm a guy who has studied bipolar for 20 years, and who knows not to go off medication. But I was in so much physical pain last year, as a result of my prescription, that I literally had bloody blisters down my body. I was covered in second degree burns. I was on the tipping point of something called Stevens-Johnson syndrome — which is a condition that only 1% of people survive — and the pain clouded my judgement. I'd managed to heal the burns to my skin through a honeycomb-based topical solution, but the nerve pain returned; it felt like knives and needles were coming from my bones and shooting through the skin! I couldn't take it anymore, and because of the pain, I went off my meds. And I didn't tell anyone.

Here's the thing though, Jas. Usually I'm a very self-aware human being, and I'm very aware of when I become manic. But this experience was different. Unlike my previous seven psych ward stays, I wasn't suicidal. Instead, I had skyrocketed into such a manic high that I was stuck there.

The thing about mania, is that it gives you a natural high that takes you to such amazing heights — but if you get too manic, it can also become very dangerous. What people don't understand, is that mania, if not checked for weeks upon end, causes akin to brain damage. The neurons and synapses are firing so quickly, and if you don't come down, you're hurting your brain in a permanent sense. That's what happened to me last year... And I'll tell you, I've not fully recovered from that manic high. It *has* impacted me. There were some days I'd turn to my wife, and ask, 'Why are you in my bed?' She would show me photos of my father, and I'd just look at them blankly and say, 'I don't know that man.' I called my best friend one day, and he couldn't even understand me. He thought it was a crank call.

After having my doctor assess me over a Zoom call, I turned to my wife and I said: "Margie, I've got to go in [to the psych ward].' In that moment, there was no other choice. Because if I didn't go in, I knew I was going to crash. If I didn't get help, I was going to further damage my brain.

Even now, with having been out of the psychiatric ward for months, I still have significant cognitive delay most days, and I find that most nights, I'm unable to verbalise and articulate myself. I remember going in front of an audience earlier this year, and asking them the same thing 15 times. *'What was I talking about? What did I just say?'* For a guy who speaks all around the world... It was devastating. I am back to a much better place now, but it did impact me greatly.

If it wasn't for my wife Margaret, I wouldn't have gotten better so many times. I know I wouldn't be here. If it wasn't for Margaret, I wouldn't be the man I am today. She really is the strongest human I've ever met. Strong mind, strong body, strong heart, strong everything... She's also incredibly gifted and incredibly beautiful. She has been there for me when I'm at the lowest of my lows, and she has helped me get back up, like Muhammad Ali, and get back into the ring and back into the fight.

JR: I think that sometimes people don't realise the important role that caregivers and partners play in the mental wellbeing of those with bipolar or a mental illness, and how easily they too can burn out while trying to be our rock. What are some of the things Margie does to 'fill her cup', so that she can give back to you?

KH: Firstly, Margie has a lot of friends that she knows she can call — anywhere from Australia to the Philippines, and all over the world.

She knows they'll be here for her any time, and talking to her friends is often her therapy. But that said, sometimes she doesn't need that. Sometimes she just needs some space, some calming music, and time to herself. That's something we can all do. As human beings we need to understand that when there is too much stimulation, we need to do some deep breathing and just have time with ourselves.

JR: As someone who is always on the go and spends most of the year travelling around the world, what are your top self-care strategies for staying mentally well?

KH: To stay on top of my brain pain, I have to do my best to stay in a routine. I eat at the same time, exercise at the same times, and have my speeches between the same times. No matter where I am in the world, I'll make sure I wake up between 4.30 and 6.30am — and every morning I start the day with foods that are anti-inflammatory, like oatmeal and fruit. After that I'll head to the gym, then get ready for my presentation, and exercise again before 5pm. And finally, every chance I can, I take the time to read about bipolar disorder. I have a Google alert on type one bipolar disorder, and it's important to me that I do the work to understand what I can bring into my routine to better my brain health.

Find out more about Kevin and Margaret Hines' work at: kevinhinesstory.com

REASONS TO LIVE...
Surviving & Thriving After Sexual or Domestic Violence

A note from Jas Rawlinson

In the past decade, I have come across more survivors of sexual and domestic assault that I could have ever believed possible. It feels as though nearly every woman I speak to — whether it be a client, friend, or acquaintance — has experienced these forms of trauma. Likewise, I have also spoken to several brave male survivors and heard of the most deeply unjust, distressing, and hurtful forms of abuse they too have been subjected to at the hands of their female partners. I've listened to stories of men who've been beaten and had their children turned against them; men who've been psychologically controlled and isolated from friends; men who've acquiesced to their partner's demands for various luxury items, only to be left broken and hurt when they ran out of money (which is a form of financial and psychological abuse). Stories like these are just a few of the reasons why I created and dedicated a domestic violence memorial in my town to both male and female survivors.

As you can likely imagine, just like the topic of child abuse I was overwhelmed with survivors willing to share their stories for this volume. To be honest, I think these chapters were the hardest for me to write, edit, and put together; perhaps because of my own experience with domestic violence, and the terror I witnessed in my home as a child.

With 1 in 4 women and 1 in 6 Aussie men subjected to emotional abuse by a current or former partner since age 15, and 1 in 6 women and 1 in 16 men experiencing physical and/or sexual violence since the same age (Australian Institute of Health and Welfare, 2018) it's fair to say that most of us would know of at least one person who has experienced these forms of trauma.

I won't spoil their stories for you, as both chapters are truly incredible in different ways, however, you might be surprised to learn that Laura and Angela are indeed best friends. Even more incredible, however, is that these two courageous women didn't meet as 'survivors.' Rather, both women became friends when they were still in abusive relationships. As you read their stories, take heart in the fact that even during their darkest hours, both Laura and Angela had each other's backs, and today, as two strong women who are free of their abusive marriages, they remain best of friends.

I cannot even begin to describe the courage needed for both of these women to not only leave their abusers, but to also share their stories with the world. This aside, I've no doubt their words will heal, inspire hope, and give comfort to many who have experienced, or are currently in, abusive relationships (whether male or female), and I want to honour that. So, thank you Laura and Angela.

Laura
(Australia)

"As we sat talking, I realised just how different this counsellor was to others I had seen over the past two decades. Instead of asking me to 'submit to my husband', she referred me to a Domestic Violence service. Imagine what this was like, after 20 years of not having one single counsellor or person in my church recommend me to an actual DV service."

"You've hit the jackpot!"

In my earliest memories, I see myself snuggled into my dad's lap, safe and protected. As mum tinkered around the kitchen, I'd breathe in the delicious aromas wafting through the room and nestle in closer as Dad's soft, gentle voice recited one of my bedtime Bible stories.

Reminiscing on this memory, I can see how truly blessed I was as a child. My parents were incredibly loving and caring, and my dad was always going above and beyond to make life fun. In fact, every year he would dress up as Santa and sneak around the house on Christmas Eve in his Father Christmas suit, knowing that even though it was late, we kids wouldn't be able to resist sneaking out to 'look for Santa'.

It's safe to say that life was pretty normal and drama-free as a child (which is why my journey as an adult will probably come as a shock to you). My teen years were a little more stressful, however, as Dad suffered a heart attack when I was just 11, and although he went on to recover, for a long time us older kids had to look after our younger siblings (as mum felt the enormity of dad not being able to work).

As I finished school, I started to think about what it was that I wanted to do for a career. Given that I'd been cutting my siblings' hair since I was 11 years old, I couldn't think of anything I'd rather do! So at age 17, I decided to switch my country life for the bright lights, culture, and endless opportunities of 'The City'. During this time I was offered a place to stay with my church youth pastor, and it was through this connection that I met the man who was to become my husband.

Tall, dark, and handsome — not to mention the son of a high-profile pastor — Damien was the best new talent to come into the church (and I wasn't the only girl to notice!). Shortly afterwards, we began dating, and within 18 months we were engaged. While we were complete opposites when it came to our personalities (he was quiet, while I was outgoing), I thought that somehow, we could make it work.

At just 23, and completely new to the world of 'relationships,' I truly thought I had found my soulmate (and the fact that he was the son of a pastor was a pretty big bonus). "Wow Laura, you've really hit the jackpot!" my Dad said to me one day, his voice full of pride.

All I could do was smile from ear to ear. I had no idea of the heartache and hell l was to go through.

Submit to your husband and forgive

In retrospect, the signs began appearing a number of months before our wedding. But the moment I truly knew something wasn't right, was after we returned home from our honeymoon. Very quickly, life became about walking on eggshells. It didn't matter if it was the sound of the vacuum or the scratch of my knife and fork as I ate dinner; everything, *anything*, made him angry. I grew to become terrified of that look in eyes.

The day that has always stuck with me the strongest, however, is the day that his mood turned from agitation to physical abuse. It was a seemingly normal day. I went to work, came home, and started getting dinner ready. All I was doing was cutting up some veggies, when Damien started complaining about me 'making too much noise.' A few seconds went by and I heard his voice again, this time commanding and full of anger. *"Laura! Stop. Making. Noise."* Fear coursed through my body and my heart began to beat faster. I backed away, retreating from the look on his face. Then, before I could even blink, he hit me. Dazed and in disbelief, shock quickly took over and I found myself barely able to move.

The next day, filled with remorse, Damien sent me a huge bouquet of flowers. "I'm so sorry, I'll never do anything like this ever again," he promised tenderly. Having never experienced domestic violence in my life, l guess it was easy to believe him. He truly sounded so sincere. However, as you can probably imagine, it was only a short amount of time before this vicious pattern began to repeat.

Over the months and years that followed, the situations were often different, and sometimes it was our walls and doors that were on the receiving end of his punches (rather than me) — but the violence was always lurking. The most terrifying part was how quickly his demeanour could switch from explosive, to terrifyingly calm. At times his voice was hushed and laden with ice, while at others, he could terrify me into silence with one glance.

You might be wondering, *'Where were his parents during all of this? Did the church know what was going on?'* This was, perhaps, one of the most traumatic parts of my 20 years of marriage — because there were many times that Damien's parents dropped in to visit us and experienced his agitation and anger first hand. I mean, it wasn't hard to spot. Yet, over and over, his mum would respond by quoting scriptures about the need for a woman to have a 'gentle and kind spirit,' or telling *me* to keep my voice down (even though I was just talking in my normal tone).

As the years rolled on, Damien's rage reached an all-time high. I never knew what he would do next. I lost count of the number of times he would stand over me raining down threats (or sometimes putting holes in the wall), and I felt like there was no one to reach out to. The worst part was, I had one of the most supportive families you could ever hope for, the type who would have done anything to get me out of there, but I was trapped. Every time they called and asked how I was, I wanted nothing more than to let myself breakdown; to tell them every awful detail and ask my dad or family to come and get me. But every time I took a call, Damien would be there listening to every word — and making sure I knew it.

By now I knew that I was in desperate need of help. *'If I can't tell my family, maybe someone at church can help me,'* I thought. So, picking up the phone one day while Damien was out, I called our church to make an appointment. Crying in fear and shame, I told this person every detail of what was going on (even today I'm too nervous to name who it was). When I finished speaking, he simply replied that he 'found it hard to believe.' "Laura, as a woman of God you must submit to your husband and forgive him 70 x 7," was all he said. This person had no idea what domestic violence was or the true terror of my home life.

If I didn't know it already, I knew it now... I was truly alone.

His entire body is hot and full of rage. Every fibre of my being prickles with adrenalin, silently pleading with me to take action. 'Run, Laura, run!' *Grabbing my purse, I take off toward the train station, constantly checking over my shoulder as my feet pound against the cement. My heart thumps so hard I'm afraid it will give out. I clutch my chest, silently willing myself to calm.* 'I've just got to get back to my family. Everything will be okay, I just need to get to my family...' *Looking wildly around the train station, I fumble in my purse. With despair, I stare at the spare change in my hand. I don't have enough money... My heart starts beating wildly again; my brain desperately searching for a new plan. Taking the money I have, I board a train to a nearby suburb where a couple from our church lives. It's the only option I have. As my whole body shakes uncontrollably, I stand before my 'friends', sharing every humiliating detail and hoping that somehow, they can help me.*

Instead, they offer a prayer and then take me back home... Back to Damien.

After everything Damien had put me through that weekend, there was nothing more terrifying than being dropped off and left to fend for myself. As I walked through the doors, shaking and petrified, he took one look at me and got straight on the phone to his dad, telling him what I'd done and that I'd been talking to someone from the congregation. On his father's instruction, we went straight down to the church for 'counselling.' I remember sitting there in his office, just feeling so terrified. Standing over me, my father-in-law looked me dead in the eye. "If you ever tell a single Pastor about this, or anyone else, that will be it for you."

Fearful of what might happen, I became even more cautious about what I did and who I spoke to. More and more, I started to withdraw inside myself.

Don't tell a single soul

From the outside I still looked like I had it all; the perfect 'family,' the perfect marriage, and a thriving new business. It was 1988 and we had just opened a hair salon — something I'd always dreamed of doing! Although the abuse at home was still a constant, the salon provided a welcome outlet for my creativity and passion. It also helped me to blackout what was being done to me at home. That said, the hair salon we opened was far grander than what I had originally anticipated, and as a result, I felt overwhelmed with pressure to make it succeed. I shouldn't have worried so much — within four years we had gone from a handful of clients to several thousand!

Despite all of my career success, 1992 was a year from hell and one of the worst years of my life. I was diagnosed with rubella, and shortly afterwards, miscarried at 12 weeks. (Just 10 days later, I was back at work — little did I know I was suffering from postnatal depression). Throughout all of this, the abuse was still a constant, although it had become less physical by this stage. (It didn't need to be, as Damien had conditioned me very well to know '*what would happen*'). Though I was still terrified, I'd tried reaching out to many counsellors, including several outside the church, but not a single one would address or validate my experiences. Burnt out from work, and mentally drained from Damien's abuse, I began to spiral downward.

Then, on August 3rd of that year, came another blow. My 24 year old sister-in-law died. We spent all week sitting by her side as she lay there on life support, and trying to come to terms with her being 'gone', felt unimaginable and horrific. The two of us had become so close over the past 10 years, and with everything else going on in my life, her death left me struggling to keep my head above water. The grief of Damien losing his sister was enormous also, and every night was spent trying desperately to console him.

The final straw came when we were recommended to see a particular marriage 'counsellor', whose 'professional opinion' was that all the problems in my marriage simply boiled down to my own issues. (I later discovered this 'counsellor' knew and approved of Damien's father). From this moment on, it was hard to see a reason to keep living. Every road led back to Damien's father, and there was not a single person who believed or validated my emotional pain. After years of being beaten down in every way, it felt as though any last flicker of hope was truly gone.

The following Monday, out of desperation, I rang one of the 'counsellors' back and begged for help, telling them very clearly that I wanted to end my life. I was told that it would be 'several weeks' before they could see me. The emotional pain l felt in this moment was like no other, and I just felt too exhausted to keep on going. All I wanted was for the nightmare to end. So, standing on the edge of the second story balcony, I made the only decision I felt I could.

I still remember the pain as I hit the tiles below; it was agonising. All I wanted was for the pain to stop. And so I tried again, this time a different way. It's not my proudest moment, and I know some may not understand why I share this so graphically, but what I want people to understand is this: the emotional pain was just *so unbearable*. It's a myth that people commit suicide just for attention. For me, I truly couldn't see another way.

'Coming to' in the emergency department, with Damien and his parents standing over me (and my body strapped tightly into a hospital harness), felt like being in a horror movie. The only thing that was worse was the news that I may never walk again. For the first three days, they just didn't know what quality of life I would have.

As I lay in bed, depressed, isolated, and unable to move an inch (let alone walk), in strolled Damien's father. Once again, I was threatened repeatedly and sworn to secrecy. I was not to speak to anyone about what had happened, he said; not even my family. And if anyone did ask? Well, I was to tell them I had fallen down the stairs.

For five weeks I stayed in the Orthopaedic ward — during which time I was unable to even shower. Whenever my family called to ask about my 'accident', all I could do was sob. I was so full of heartache and grief at what my life had become. Eventually, though, my family did find out the truth. I still remember that day so clearly. After weeks on my own, I remember looking up one morning to see my sister walking toward my bed. I thought I must have been hallucinating! "Is that really you?" I asked, touching her face and arms repeatedly. For the first time in so long, I finally felt safe. After this, my other sister arrived, nursing me back to health and helping me to learn how to walk.

By now I well and truly understood that I had been abused for far too long, and so I made the decision to move back to my family home. As you can probably imagine, Damien was extremely remorseful, and finally, he began to treat me like a human being. It might sound stupid, but with so much family around me, I thought it would stay this way. The thing about living with an abuser, though, is that it's just a matter of time before the storm clouds reappear…

Lies, lows, and light at the end of the tunnel

In 1994, surrounded by my family, I gave birth to my first child. After being told just two years prior that I would have back pain for the rest of my life, and that children were out of the question, I was overjoyed and in love with this new little life before me. (My back had also fully healed!). Three years later I gave birth to our second precious child. Life was fantastic! Some months later, Damien was offered a contract interstate, and with the promise that it would only be for a few months, I agreed that we'd all go together.

Things were okay for a while, but by 2003, I had hit rock bottom. With Damien working 10-hour days, and the day-to-day exhaustion of looking after two children while still dealing with his abuse, my body and soul were worn out. Every day was spent racking my brain for any possible way to get myself and my children out. But it felt like there just wasn't one.

Deeply depressed and anxious, I once again found myself in that place of mental and physical exhaustion. I knew I just couldn't go on anymore. And so, on a bright and sunny day in 2003, I got in the car and drove out to a nearby mountain. Again, my plan was to take my life. Turning on the radio to fill the silence, I continued up the mountain. Then it happened. The words that would change the course of my life forever…

"Don't make a permanent decision for a temporary situation."

What?! Turning my attention to the radio, I began listening intently. "Suicide is never the answer. Please, reach out for help," begged the radio host. He was running a suicide prevention segment. Very carefully, I pulled over to the side of the road and sat there quietly, my body shaking like a leaf. In that moment, all I could hear in my mind was my son's voice. "Stop crying mummy, it's going to be okay." I could picture his little hands on my face, wiping away the tears; his soft voice, so gentle and innocent, urging me on: "Stop crying mummy, it's going to be okay." That was when I knew I couldn't go through with my plan. I just couldn't. So, carefully, and slowly, I turned on the engine and drove home. The moment I arrived, I walked straight to the phone, picked it up, and immediately made an appointment with a psychologist. It was the call that saved my life.

Over the next six months, I worked with this psychologist on a weekly basis. (I had to carefully and strategically take money from my grocery funds in order to pay for these sessions and keep them secret from Damien). As we progressed, he explained how strongly my core beliefs had been eroded, and that it would take time to rewire my thought patterns. After several months of using cognitive behavioural therapy, I was able to rebuild my core beliefs to a level where, for the first time in decades, I could finally *see* who I was. This time, when the next wave of abuse came, I felt stronger. I *was* stronger. So, while the kids were at school one day, I packed three suitcases and arranged to go to a girlfriend's place. Then I picked the kids up and took them back to her house, where I knew we would be safe. For added protection, I also left my car in her garage. With her help, we went to the police station together, where I wrote a 10-page Domestic Violence Order of Abuse from 1984 to 2003. "Why did you keep going back?" asked the police officer, as I scrawled page after page. "Well, the church counsellors said I had to stay and work on my marriage," I answered honestly. To say she was dumbfounded would be an understatement!

When I arrived home to my family, all I had with me were those three suitcases. I still remember the day Missions Australia arrived on my doorstep with mattresses, blankets, food, and a promise to organise a fridge and a washing machine. To think that someone could so selflessly want to help me was *unfathomable*. Tears of gratitude spilled down my face. To me, this was *true* Christianity.

Still, Damien wouldn't let me go. I had only just begun to make a new life for myself when suddenly the legal letters began arriving. Damien had a solicitor, and according to the letter, it was an order that I 'return home'. Over the coming months, he manipulated me into believing I had to abide by what the solicitor was saying — when in actual fact, this was a lie. As soon as I returned, the verbal and emotional abuse restarted, and I felt myself beginning to slide back down into the slippery grip of depression. On the recommendation of one of my friends, who I knew I could trust, I called a female counsellor at a nearby church and asked if I could see her. As we sat talking later that week, I realised just how different this counsellor was to others I had seen over the past two decades. For example, instead of justifying the abuse, she validated what I was saying. Instead of asking me to 'submit to my husband', she referred me to a Domestic Violence service. Imagine what this was like, after 20 years of not having one single counsellor or person in my church recommend me to an actual DV service!

Soon afterwards, I completed a 12-week recovery program (which I cannot recommend more highly) and continued to see my counsellor, who gradually helped me put into action a safety plan. (As many who've walked this journey will know, this is typically the most dangerous time a victim can leave.) I also began to tackle my depression through writing. Whether it was words of gratitude or diary entries of what was happening at home, it was a way to record my thoughts and get the junk out of my head. As I read through the many chapters of my life story, I became more clear-headed and able to stop negative thoughts.

Rising from the ashes

After so many years of abuse I finally grew strong enough to begin court proceedings, and to tell Damien that it was over. This time, for good. Unbelievably, within just eight weeks, he had moved out. In time, with freedom from the daily abuse, I was able to find a new home for myself and my children to begin our new life.

I turned 50 in my new little place and my family threw a party to help me celebrate new beginnings. I felt like a completely different person! Yes, I had virtually no money or possessions, but I was free from abuse.

Life has taught me so much, and despite all the pain, I know for sure that I am here by the Grace of God to help as many people as I can, and to encourage those who are still stuck in abusive relationships to believe that it's possible to start a new life and make a full recovery. Comprehensive education around domestic violence is desperately needed in our communities — particularly schools and churches. There are a lot of people out there who need a safe haven to escape to, and often that's a church. I am not saying all churches are bad, and my faith in God has helped me through so many hard times, but religious leaders need to be professionally educated on what domestic violence and mental illness are, and to stop being complicit in a victim's continued abuse.

There were so many fallacies I was told during my two decades in an abusive relationship. Perhaps the most common, was to 'stay' for my children. I can tell you right now, there are few things more damaging to your child than being exposed to abuse — mine included. I was very fortunate to come across an organisation called *Circuit Breaker*, who provided amazing support to my son at age 12. Every two weeks they would come out to spend time and chat with him about different topics, including expression and management of anger. I am so grateful that I have been able to help him break the cycle!

To those reading who are currently trapped in an abusive relationship, I want to say this: domestic violence is not only physical. Intimidation, isolation, minimising and denying feelings, use of blame, emotional/spiritual/economical abuse, withholding children as a form of power, and coercion and threats, are all forms of domestic abuse. Please reach out to the people who are waiting to help you — if you have good friends, lean on them! If you don't, find a professional. It may take a long time to grow strong enough to leave, but with professional help, your journey can be so much shorter than mine. I am forever indebted to my family and friends who have been a rock throughout my hard times, and who I partly owe my life to. I have also chosen to keep close to those friends who offered a hand; the friends who listened compassionately and who I knew would answer anytime I called.

Being able to look at myself in the mirror and know that my story has helped someone else, shows me that the pain and hell I went through was not in vain. Writing and getting my story out there gives me a reason to live one more day, over and over again. Yes, I am still healing, but I can now see how far I've come. I am strong and I have a voice; a voice that hopes to reach many others who feel trapped. A voice that aims to show, through my words, that they don't have to live what I have.

A note from Jas Rawlinson

When Laura first approached me to write her story, she was sure this was the time to break her silence and share her story under her real name. She was keen to put a face to her story and be validated. However, after much discussion, and to make sure she was safe from her abusers, we decided it would be best to keep her identity hidden. One day Laura hopes to tell her full story under her real name. She currently lives in Australia and enjoys time with her family and getting back to the roots of where she grew up.

Angela McFarlane
Melbourne, VIC (Australia)

"Giving this letter to you dear Angela, I want you to know this. Your journey is not one of defeat. You've stood on the ledge of darkness, within an inch of losing your life, but you've rebuilt yourself into a 'whole' woman; a woman with such resilience and determination that life cannot beat you. Yes, it might knock you flat on your ass at times! But every time it does, you dust yourself off and pick yourself up."

A letter to my younger self...

Dear Angela,
I know you are so confused right now; trying desperately to be so big and invisible at the same time. All you want to do is protect yourself, Nathan, and Mum. But it's so frightening. And who wouldn't be terrified? After all, my dear child, you are only three years old.

It is so noisy, Jack yelling. His voice so loud, scary, and threatening. The only sound worse is that of Mum's voice as Jack's fists connect with her face, her head, her body... anywhere he can reach in his fury. I can see you doing your best, trying so hard to keep your baby brother quiet. It would be an almost impossible feat for anyone, let alone a small child. Nathan's constant wailing and shrieking makes your ears hurt. Tears well in your eyes. Pain builds in your throat. You're fighting so hard against those feelings inside; the pressure of trying to be so brave, while wishing there was someone to protect you. Someone to keep you safe and tell you everything's going to be okay... Because this is not okay.

Being quiet is the single most terrifying thing at this moment — but it's the safest option. If Nathan doesn't stop screaming, Jack (his biological father, your stepfather) will very likely hit him. He hates his son with a passion that's hard to comprehend. Yet, even from the very beginning he never liked Nathan. So many times he would punch Mum in the stomach, knowing she was pregnant; knowing he was putting his son at risk. He just didn't care.

I can see you crouching on the floor in terrified silence, watching in terror as the black shadows dart backwards and forwards across the living room. Sometimes you sit with Nathan on the lounge while the violence unfurls, or sometimes the floor, but it doesn't matter where you are; the fear is always the same. No place is safe, except for one that's hidden. Wardrobes. Cupboards.

Anywhere you can squeeze your body into while Jack gives Mum her 'daily' beating.

I know you aren't able to understand this just yet, dear Ange, but none of this was your fault. It wasn't your job to protect your baby brother. It wasn't your job to check on Mum and ask if she was okay. As a little girl, the only 'job' you should have had, was to laugh and play; to be safe, loved, protected, and nurtured. Not to be terrified all the time. It makes me sad to tell you this, but it won't be until the physical violence reaches you, dear one, that your mother will finally grow strong enough to leave Jack.

I still remember that day; the way he called you to him while you were playing outside. The way you stood there, paralysed with fear, before finally willing yourself to walk those terrifying steps across the yard. I remember the absolute shock and soul-crushing hurt, as his fist punched straight into your tiny forehead. Then I remember your mother and her face; the realisation dawning that the fear of leaving, was no longer greater than the fear of staying.

It will be on this day, as Jack sleeps, that your mother quickly packs a bag and takes you to safety. She hurries as fast as she can, knowing that Jack will kill her if he sees what is happening. But as you all creep silently out the door, she realises the problem. There aren't enough hands to carry your bags, as well as both you and Nathan. But in that moment, a slither of hope appears. A miracle. As a young boy rides past on his bicycle, she seizes the opportunity to save you. "Please, take my daughter on your bike, take her to this address," she pleads, giving him the details for your aunt's house down the road. She hands him a dollar and waves you onward, following in the distance with Nathan.

Being caught in a cycle of domestic violence is a hard one to break free from. But you're too young to understand this just yet.

It makes you sad to find out that Mum thought it was 'normal' to have bruises on her face; that often, she would just 'wait' for the third punch — because after that she couldn't feel it anymore. "Oh, Jack gave it me," she'd say casually whenever asked by our local shopkeeper what happened to her face. She believed it was all normal, Ange. Truly, she did.

Many years later, you'll ask why she waited until this moment to leave. The sad truth is, that until then, she thought that so long as he was hitting her, she could defend herself — completely misunderstanding that the damage had already been done to all of you. I wish she had been able to leave earlier, because then, dear Ange, maybe you would have been sheltered from the devastating abuse that was yet to come. But as you read this, hold onto these six words: *none of it was your fault*. And no matter what life throws at you, you will find a way to rise above.

You're 16 years old now, dear Ange. It's been many years since Jack left, and yet, you still hold a wariness within your heart toward men. I understand; and given all you've experienced, it makes sense. Yet, even with these scars, I know that you still look for the best in people — and that, my dear one, is a gift. I know that very soon, you'll wish you were harder, colder, less trusting. You'll blame yourself for being so naive, for not seeing the dark intent hidden inside some people. But ask yourself this: how could you have known what they were planning? No, no one could have imagined such a betrayal — least of all, that it could come from your best friend.

Wild, carefree, and with no parental guidelines, Sandra is the kind of girl who does what she likes, whenever she wants. And for a shy and naive 16-year-old like you, who always tries to do her best by others and play by the rules, it's alluring. So when Sandra invites you to hang out one night, you say yes in a heartbeat. You've already met some of her friends the night before, so you don't think much of it — except that it seems weird for a teenage girl to be spending time with 25-year-old men. After all, you've never even had a boy call your home phone before — let alone, *hang out* together.

Deep in your gut, a little voice of warning sounds, cautioning you to be careful, to never put your trust in a man the way that Sandra does... The way Mum did. But you figure as long as you stick with Sandra — your friend — everything will be fine. As far as you're concerned, she can chase boys if she likes, but you'll stick to talking with your girlfriends.

The only problem is, when you get to Sandra's friend's house it's just her and two men. Anxiety and distrust immediately begin to flower inside your stomach. Being alone with two men in their twenties isn't the norm for you — and even Sandra can see how uncomfortable you are. But for some reason, she makes out like your feelings are irrational. As you look to her for support, you hear a noise; a male voice calling your name from one of the bedrooms. "Hey Ange, come in here for a sec." I still remember the feeling, the uneasiness that spasmed in your stomach as the warning bell sounded louder. 'Run,' it urges. '*Do not* go in there.' You so desperately want to leave, to go home and climb into the safe warmth of your bed. But Sandra wants you to stay, smiling at you in that sickeningly 'reassuring' way. "Don't be scared Ange, it's all fine. Go in, I'll be right here."

So, slowly, anxiously, you walk into the room. In an instant, you take it all in. His light blue nightshirt. The sickening *'click,'* as the door behind you closes and locks. The strangling panic clawing its way up your throat. Sandra's laughter trailing in from the lounge room. His words, "Take your clothes off, get on the bed." The truth — that this was all a setup. As I recount this memory, as I write our story, I still feel tears pricking my eyes. No 16-year-old, no person, should ever be betrayed and hurt in such a way, dear Ange.

In this moment, Ange, you will be forced to make a decision that no one should ever be faced with: the decision to fight back or to focus on getting out of that room as safely as possible. (Everyone always says they'd fight back in a situation like that, but until you're faced with such terror, you can never truly know what choice you would make.) And let me tell you, fighting back was definitely your first choice — even though you weigh only 37kg. You are desperate to do anything to try and stop what's about to happen; but you also know that any act of protest could be more dangerous than the terrible predicament you are in right now. There is also the fear that if you scream, there could be two men in that room. So you choose to fight for your life in the only way possible; by not making a sound. Your childhood survival triggers kick in. *'Being quiet is the single most terrifying thing at this moment — but it's the safest option'*. With a level of strength and courage that will astound you in years to come, you turn your focus to the digital clock on the bedside table, tears flowing down your face as you will yourself to stare at those numbers. 20 long minutes pass. 1200 seconds of pushing yourself to hold on a little longer. And then, finally, it is over. You've survived. You can leave.

For many years afterwards, you'll struggle to believe that the rape was not your fault. *If only I hadn't been there in the first place. If only I had tried to fight back.* I remember all the thoughts; all the self-hatred and painful lies.

It's hard for people to understand the levels of shame, anger, and self-loathing that sprout within your mind after something as traumatic as rape. The physical pain is one thing, the emotional destruction is another. It's not just a physical assault on your body; it's an assault on your soul. You'd think an 'expert' would understand this, but the judgement you faced when you did finally reach out to a support service — after five days of constant bleeding and agony — was incredulous. *"You stupid girl, why would you put yourself in that situation?"* That was all that was said. I wanted to hold you so tightly, to calm the uncontrollable shaking and furnace of tears. *Didn't she know how hard that was to even pick up the phone?* Even though she was a stranger, you hated that woman for a long, long time.

Getting through those days and months after the assault, often made you feel like an emotional yo-yo. For days at a time, you'd be consumed by nothing other than rage and disgust (*What makes someone think they can take without consent something that is supposed to be treasured!?*), while on others, you were bogged down by soul-crushing sadness (*How could a person be so callous to just go on with their life as if nothing happened?!*). And above all, you had to live through a daily, deeply ingrained, sense of fear. The thought of going to the police, having to find a man whose name you don't even know, being faced with the trauma of going back to 'that' house, worrying about the judgement of your friends and family…The thought of telling Mum… It was all too much to face. And that okay, Ange. That's okay. After all, we both know Mum couldn't have been there for you even if she'd tried.

There will be many days where the desire for isolation will be all-encompassing, Ange. But I want you to know that no matter what that man thought, he was no hero. There is nothing heroic about locking a young girl in a room and forcing such horror upon her. He was a grown man. A man who knew you were a child and that you couldn't fight back. In that moment, you made the only decision you felt you could, and you got yourself out of that room alive. There's so much bravery and resilience within you, my wee one, and it's going to take time to find it. But it's there. I promise you, it is. It may flicker and fade at times, but no one can extinguish it unless you give them the power to. I want you to fight, Ange. Through every painful day that comes. Don't let your survival be for nothing, beautiful.

You're just 18 years old when you first meet your future husband, David. Quiet-natured with a beautiful smile and deep brown eyes, you fall in love with him instantly. In fact, he reminds you of Richard Gere! (Something that makes all your girlfriends super jealous.) He's also charming, attentive, and thoughtful — all things the hurt little girl inside of you craves. The beautiful words whispered in your ears fall like soft, silken drops, laden with promises of love and safety.

Having never had a healthy male role model, it's impossible for you to see the difference between genuine unselfish love, and toxic obsession. Your childhood set you up perfectly for the abusive relationship you were to enter. And you weren't the only one he fooled, Ange. Even today, many people close to you still struggle to believe the truth.

On February 25th 1989, the big day arrives. And then, suddenly, your 'perfect man' begins to change. You see, domestic violence is an insidious monster, Ange. Right now you're still in the honeymoon phase — you haven't seen what I have — so you truly believe David loves you and just wants what's best. But what is coming, Ange, isn't love. Week-long arguments and constant accusations of cheating, unhealthy obsessions with where you are at all times, keeping tabs on your call history and phone bills, policing the way you speak and what you wear, forcing you to end friendships… This isn't 'David just being a bit of a jerk.' It's so much more than 'bad behaviour,' Ange.

When you finally see his behaviour for what it is, the truth is almost too hard to face. The entrenched scars from David's emotional abuse are one thing, but the internal betrayal is what hurts most; the feeling that you've let yourself down, that you've broken the promise you made as a little girl… The promise to never allow anyone to hurt you in the ways that Mum was.

I know it's difficult to hear this right now, but the only person who failed you was David. Your line in the sand was good wee one. You needed to protect yourself. If only you'd had someone to warn you about the signs of emotional abuse, to teach you how to draw that line in the sand so much earlier on, you would have known it was okay to leave before the physical violence started. Because, eventually, it will become physical.

Even then, so many 'friends' will remain under David's spell — including when he stalks you at church or your local gym. Hearing people's excuses is like being abused all over again. *"It's not like he hit you Ange, it was just a shove." "Ange, he said he's sorry, just forgive him." "But he's such a nice guy!"* It's the kind of thing that makes you want to scream!

As you grow more determined to get help, you'll spend a long time feeling like you're walking this journey alone, like everyone is judging you. You'll try to talk to your church about it, but frustratingly, they will choose not to 'see' the truth. In the end, though, you'll realise that it's not about them. Getting out, leaving, will be a decision you make for you and your children. In fact, it's only when you have your own babies that all the pieces of the puzzle finally come together.

In the years to come, as you look down at your beautiful children — who are just three, and one — playing and being the little kids they were meant to be, that's when it finally hits you. The realisation that these tiny bodies, these incredibly vulnerable humans, are just like you and Nathan all those years ago. Yet, even still, the understanding that you need to leave this abusive, volatile marriage won't be fully realised in this moment; it will take time. Eventually though, you'll grow strong enough to leave for good and break the cycle, so your dear children can grow up without ever knowing what it's like to be so petrified and so vulnerable. You'll give them the protection and nurturing they deserve; the life you never had.

Many people have no clue how hard it is to leave a violent relationship. The courage and inner strength it takes is enormous. Losing everything — from your home, to friends and family — is devastating. Seeing your children brainwashed by your abuser and hearing your son tell you, "Don't bother coming to my formal Mum, you don't deserve to be there," is a pain that is almost too much to bear. But when you throw chronic pain into the mix (which developed after your rape) it's no wonder so many people give up. One of the hardest parts for you Ange, comes down to the fact that you *are* so strong. Because of your high pain tolerance and ability to push on even when you're in so much physical pain, people don't realise how much you're hurting. That's why you've got to let them in; you've got to speak out. If you keep putting your mask on, no one will ever be there when you find the strength to leave.

Lean on Laura — you've been friends for so long now, and you know she understands. After all, she's been in the same situation. You guys have each other's backs, and together, you'll come out the other side. Life is so much better with supportive friends — don't shut them out, Ange. And please, if no one else is there for you, fight for yourself and your freedom. It comes down to you, my dear girl. You have to break the cycle.

It will feel agonisingly pointless at times; like you're not getting anywhere. But just as a forest regrows after a fire, so too will your courage. Hold on for dear life with everything you have when the dark times hit, Ange; because I promise you, one day you'll see a light at the end of the tunnel. (A very long tunnel, but still!) When you find that spark of light, run toward it; let its soothing, calming, and warm love soak over you.

In your journey to freedom, one of the things that will help you most is taking part in a 12-week domestic violence support program. To feel your confidence slowly piecing itself back together, will be more valuable than you could ever imagine! Rediscovering who you are without David, will give you the strength you need to begin rebuilding.

Will life be a piece of cake once you leave? No. But every one of us has our own struggles Ange, and through it all, you'll find the inner strength to keep going. True friends will reveal themselves, while the fake ones will slither away. Slowly, your son Daniel will come back to you. Sadly, your daughter will take more time. But for now, hold onto hope; because right now, freedom — life — is enough.

It has been over 20 years now. 11 years since David left. There are still days that are hard. Long lists of medication to keep up with; chronic pain and brain fog. Having to stop work at 47 was not in your life plan. But you've come to love life, even with the dark days.

It has taken you a long time to understand the connection between stress and your physical pain, but as an older woman, you've learned how to set boundaries to protect yourself. In fact, you'd be surprised to know what a sassy woman you've turned into. Nobody messes with Ange these days! I think that's one of the things I've loved watching most during your journey. That, and your determination to fight for the life you deserve.

Giving this letter to you wee Angela, I want you to know this. Your journey from that of a small and vulnerable child, through to an adult who has faced more than her fair share of tragedy, pain, rejection, and broken heartedness, is not one of defeat. Yes, you will face more trauma than many encounter in their lifetime, but the purpose of this letter is to show you, and others, that healing, restoration, and self-forgiveness (yes, truly) are not only possible, but attainable. How can I say that? Because I have witnessed it for myself. Many, many tears will fall along the way. But with the help of understanding counsellors, guidance, prayer, support, and love — and the tiniest of baby steps — you'll come out the other side.

Despite all the pain you've been through, you've proven to yourself that you *can* and *will* survive. You've stood on the ledge of darkness, within an inch of losing your life to the incredible depths of grief and sorrow. But from these ashes, you've rebuilt yourself into a 'whole' woman; a woman with such resilience and determination that life *cannot* beat you. Yes, it might knock you flat on your ass at times! But every time it does, you dust yourself off and pick yourself up. You've learned what a healthy relationship looks like, how it feels, and exactly what you deserve.

The best thing I can leave with you my beautiful girl, is to tell you that you will be okay. You can and will survive. One day you will feel happy; you'll feel reconstructed, as though your mind, heart, and your very soul have been remodelled. A corny saying, I guess.... But have hope, dear Angela. New beginnings will come.

You are loved, you are valued, and you are never truly alone.

ANGELA MCFARLANE is a survivor of domestic violence and rape, who is passionate about using her voice to empower others who are trapped in abusive relationships. Based in Victoria, she spends her spare time reading, baking, hunting for op shop gems, or enjoying a good cup of tea with some dark chocolate on the side.

REASONS TO LIVE
Surviving & Thriving with Chronic Illness

A note from Jas Rawlinson

In 2009 I developed a chronic pain condition that would haunt me for the following three years. As I shared in volume one of 'Reasons to Live,' it was a strange disorder, and one which no doctor seemed able to diagnose or treat. On my best days, it was a mere ache or throbbing pain that settled in my legs; at worst, it was a sharp, shooting pain that speared my fingers, arms, face, or legs with a bite to rival that of fire ant. Thankfully, I could usually distract myself from it while I was busy. Night time, however, was a different story. As soon as I got into bed and my mind was switching off, I would be acutely aware of the pain, which would then get worse the more I thought about it!

For three long and awful years, I battled not only the physical pain but also the mental. I also became an insomniac. Depression crept back into my life, and I felt like a freak; a burden to everyone around me. It was a key factor as to why I moved away from home in 2009, ended a relationship that was heading toward marriage, and started a fresh life. I just wanted to be alone. In many ways I got lucky, because after three years, I finally developed some mindfulness techniques that helped me stop noticing the pain — and miraculously it eventually left! Not everyone with chronic pain is that blessed, and for that reason, I am always in awe of anyone who battles this type of war on the daily (just like Justine, the woman whose story you're about to read).

I first became aware of the hell that is 'transvaginal mesh surgery' in 2016, while interviewing journalist and former Australian Senator, Derryn Hinch. It's a device that has since destroyed the lives of thousands of people around the world (mostly women), and has since forced the Australian Government to make a formal apology. As Derryn explained to me during our interview: '[Transvaginal mesh] is as big a thing for Australian women, as Thalidomide was in the 1950s and 60s.'

To give you some context, the surgery involves the use of a mesh-like netting, which is inserted into the pelvis or bladder, often to fix incontinence or pelvic organ prolapse post-childbirth. At times it is also used on male hernia patients. However, as has since been discovered in more recent years, this is a device that embeds itself into the tissue of the patient and then begins to break down (this is where the hell begins). Many victims of this device report being unable to urinate, enjoy sex, or even walk without excruciating pain. According to a 2018 BBC article (*Vaginal mesh implants: Australia apologises for 'decades of pain'*) it was estimated that up to 8000 women may have been impacted.

Justine's story of having this device implanted, and then having her life fall apart over the next decade, is one that is truly shocking. Yet, what is even more so, is the fact that she is the only woman I've ever heard of who has managed to regain quality of life after surviving this botched procedure. She endured a level of pain most of us will never know, lost many friendships/relationships, and through it all, was treated by medical professionals as if the pain was 'all in her head.'

Without spoiling her story, I want you to keep in mind while reading Justine's chapter that not only did she find the strength to survive the horrors inflicted on her body, but she also discovered several tools and solutions that saved her life, and now help her 'function at about 80%.'

Survivors of chronic pain truly are warriors, and Justine is one of the sassiest, straight-shooting, resilient Queens I've ever met! Helping Justine to write her story of finding her reasons to live was unbelievably harrowing, yet also an absolute honour.

If you struggle with chronic pain, or know someone who does, please read and pass this story on — because those in pain need our support, empathy, and above all, love.

Justine Watson
Sydney, NSW (Australia)

"I'm still watching my 'life movie' play out. I don't know if I'll one day be able to live pain-free, enjoy pleasurable sex, and live as a fully-functioning member of society… To not have to worry about my future and all I've lost, or the damage inflicted on my poor body. But I'm grateful to have some of my life back, and I count myself as one of the lucky ones."

When life goes belly up, you tend to think about what it was that led you to that moment.

For me, it was one single moment in time. One conversation, during a girl's trip to Bali for my 40th birthday. A night of cocktails, inappropriate jokes, and snorts of laughter between friends. It was a trip that changed my life and led me down a path of chronic health problems, unimaginable physical pain, and shattered relationships. It was a decision that, in the last few years, took away my will to live.

All because of one surgery. One 'quick fix' that was meant to make my life easier, but instead, almost killed me. A surgery that has destroyed the lives of tens of thousands of women around the world, and in some cases, succeeded in taking away their will to live.

Until recently, I truly didn't believe I'd ever survive to tell my story, yet here I am, still fighting and more determined than ever to have my voice heard.

But before I tell you about my journey through the hell that is pelvic mesh surgery, I need to go back to the start…

Part one: escape to Australia

With suitcase in hand, $1000 pounds in my purse, and the steely determination of a 21-year-old 'Brummie' girl, I arrived in Sydney in July of 1991. My trip across the ocean to visit the far-away beauty of Australia was only ever meant to be a holiday; a welcome escape from the stress, anxiety, and trauma that I experienced throughout my childhood in the UK. But once I stepped foot in Sydney, I knew I'd never go back.

Growing up in the outskirts of Birmingham, I guess you could say that life looked very pretty from the outside. Behind closed doors, however, things were very different. One of my earliest memories is of me around the age of three, my nappy rubbing a blister against my legs as I clambered up the cupboard in an attempt to get food for my brother and I. As I later learned, this was the first of many times that Mum left Dad.

From the very start, my parents were an inappropriate match. Mum was middle class, while Dad was working class. Mum idolised the 'dream' of marriage; she wanted the 'two kids, a house and a husband.' But as she found, reality didn't match her vision. Having two kids within 15 months of each other is a challenge of its own — let alone adding that to the mix of her already-existing mental health issues.

As for Dad? Well, let's just say he wasn't backwards in coming forwards when he smelled bullshit. He was very stern and a bit socially awkward — definitely not a 'let's talk about our feelings' kind of father. Like most men in that era, he'd been raised with pretty rigid stereotypes of how men and women should behave. (If his slippers and scotch weren't placed in waiting for him at the end of the day, there was hell to pay — I'll leave it at that).

That said, there were a lot of things about Dad that I really admired, and throughout my life, he's been the only one who's stepped up for me over and over again. I really felt for him during those years after Mum left him for another man. As a then 11-year-old girl, it was hard to watch him fall apart. To witness the devastation it caused and see him turn to alcohol — while being helpless to do anything — caused a lot of anxiety. Many times I'd watch him go through a whole litre of scotch during an eight-hour work day, just trying to numb the pain.

Yes, Dad was abrupt and stern, but I don't think he was a bad father. Even in the midst of his depression and alcoholism after Mum left, he always made sure our bills were paid on time. I feel that, within his capacity, he did a profoundly good job. That said, none of this made life any less difficult for me.

To my peers, everything still looked rather care-free and upper-middle class, but in reality, it was filled with unpredictability and fear. 'Growing up with a knot in my stomach,' is how I've often described it. I was always on edge, waiting to see who was going to 'need' something from me. As a child, you don't have the mental capacity to make sense of this constant state of unpredictability, and for me, all that anxiety manifested itself in pretty damaging ways.

On top of all of this, I was also unknowingly dealing with dyslexia — which would explain why I didn't do so well academically. Being tall and skinny, I was drawn toward things like modelling, but as you can imagine, this also set me up for a lot of bullying. Between my learning disability, Dad's breakdown, Mum attempting suicide when I was 15, and trying to cope with my step-brothers and their father (let's just say there were things going on I would prefer to forget), there was not one place where I felt truly safe. It felt like I was living life at a 'slow burn' — thrown in the frying pan and left to sizzle away. No matter which way life flipped me, I knew I'd be left with a scar.

Throughout all of the drama and stress, somehow I kept it all together, and after finishing school at age 16, I decided I wanted to try my hand at hairdressing. After some time, however, I realised it wasn't for me. Deep down, I wanted to be seen as more than just 'pretty;' I wanted to prove that I was actually intelligent as well. So at age 19, I entered university as a mature-age student. While I still hadn't dealt with the trauma I'd been through, I guess you could say I was doing pretty well at life. I had escaped, and knowing the Government would provide me financial assistance to study and live away from home was a massive relief.

As you can probably imagine, however, all that trauma had to come out sometime. You can only hold the flood back for so long, and when I became involved in an abusive relationship during university, everything came crashing down. On that day, as I lay at the bottom of a staircase, disgusting words from my boyfriend raining down upon my bruised body, I knew deep within my soul that I just couldn't deal with life anymore.

Soon afterwards, I checked myself into a private rehabilitation facility for mental health support, where I stayed for the next month. In truth, this was the best thing I could have done for myself — although, probably not for the reasons you're thinking. I don't want to sound callous, but it didn't take me long to realise I was the sanest person in there, and I really didn't have much to worry about! (Living alongside someone who set fire to themselves will sort you out pretty quickly!) I realised that in order to thrive, all I really needed was to get away from the toxic people in my life. I just needed to be away from my family.

And so it was, in 1991, that I arrived 'Down Under.' For a Brit like me, Sydney was about the furthest away I could go. And that suited me just fine.

From the moment I arrived, Sydney was my kind of place. Every day on the way to work I'd see the familiar architecture of the Harbour Bridge coming into view and pinch myself. *Was I really here? Had I finally found a place where I could be free and at peace?* Deep inside, I knew I had finally found 'home' — and in that moment, I knew I had to find a way to turn my 'holiday' into something more permanent.

After selling my car I was still short on cash, so I got busy applying for any job I could get. For that first year, I worked as a receptionist in a brothel (they tried constantly to lure me into 'jumping the fence' — I declined). It was eye-opening to say the least, but it did at least allow me to stay in Australia.

At age 24, I gave birth to my first child — a colicky, nine-pound baby boy with the lungs of an adult. Oh, how he could scream! It was a very difficult start to motherhood, and when his dad left six weeks later, suddenly I found myself back in the 'frying pan' of life again.

One day, while looking into my son's tearful face, his skin-prickling screams bouncing off the walls, I had a life-changing moment of clarity. *'Surely there has got to be a better way for me to live,'* I thought desperately. *'I've got to step up my game. I'm sick of just existing, I want to live!'*

Inspired by a deep desire to change the course of my life, I began gravitating toward personal development, and soon afterwards, started a course in counselling. Doing this as a single mum with a toddler was pretty tough, but what it afforded me was priceless. To be seen and heard for the first time in my life, and to have the tools to tackle life without burning out, was invaluable. To this day, my counselling teacher is still one of my dearest friends.

Armed with a newfound sense of purpose, I felt ready to tackle the world. I had a job I loved, and the tools to make better life decisions. Life continued on in its busy fashion, with more challenges to come (including raising an autistic son as my next gift), but I was coping. I thought I could handle anything life threw at me.

Honestly, I had no idea what was yet to come…

Part two: it's all in your head

It was 2010. I'd just turned 40 and life was pretty good. Raising two boys, mostly on my own, had been tough — particularly with my youngest son having autism spectrum disorder. But I'd made it through, and for the first time ever my life path felt like it was about to hit cruise control.

Except for one little problem, that is. Specifically, the embarrassing little thing that kept happening every time I went to the gym. (Or laughed too hard!) Yes, after the birth of two very large baby boys, I experienced the all too common symptoms of stress urinary incontinence. To be honest, though, I wasn't too bothered by it. I was too busy caring for a special needs child, along with my clients, to worry about a bit of leakage! However, my friends weren't as relaxed (no pun intended!) as I was about 'the situation' — something that became very evident after a few too many cocktails and inappropriate jokes during a girls' trip to Bali.

"Justine, you know there's something really simple you can do about that," my friends chimed in. "You don't need to suffer with wetting yourself all the time!"

'Simple' and 'quick' were the words used to describe transvaginal mesh surgery (or pelvic organ prolapse surgery, as it's also known). Essentially, it's a 20-minute procedure where a synthetic mesh-like 'net' is placed inside your pelvis (under the urethra) to stop urine leakage and 'solve' the incontinence.

Personally, I didn't think my little problem really warranted surgery, but after some thought, I figured there was no harm in finding out more about it. So, before the year was out, I made an appointment.

Looking back, it's absolutely insane how it all happened. I was never shown the mesh or given any information. Not a single person explained that this was a permanent medical device designed never to be removed — or that it created scar tissue and inflammation when placed in the body. At no point did the surgeon explain that it was made from polypropylene (aka, the same material plastic chairs are made from) and that if it didn't go to plan, my life would become a medical hell. Had I been given this information, I would have run a mile!

After my first consult, I decided to seek out a second opinion, eventually making an appointment with a doctor recommended to me (who was also a parent to an autistic child). Prior to this moment, a little voice of doubt had been niggling within me, but when I met this surgeon I immediately pushed it away. On the spot, I trusted him. Why? Well, for those of us who care for special needs children, there's a real sense of comradery that forms between us, and naively, I thought that this doctor would have my best interests at heart. It may sound strange, but I trusted him.

So, without any further thought, I had the surgery. And that was when my life fell apart.

Vomiting in the car park, I stumbled home with the help of a friend and crawled up the stairs on my hands and knees. It was a steaming 40-degree Sydney day, and the overwhelming heat, combined with the bile bubbling in my mouth, was absolute torture. I had just had my pelvic surgery, and I felt absolutely horrendous.

Dragging myself into bed, I told myself I just needed to 'sleep it off.' But the sickness didn't pass. Even worse, was that within just a few short months, I began to notice the return of my incontinence. I remember walking into my three-month check-up and asking my surgeon what was going on, but even he admitted he was at a loss to understand why it had returned. That was the extent of his 'advice.'

Over the next few months, I began to wonder what was happening. I just didn't feel myself. I was constantly fatigued (even more so than I expected, given my career and motherly duties), and I kept getting urinary tract infections. My stomach was constantly upset and bloated by everything I ate, and I had multiple symptoms I just couldn't explain — nor could any doctor I consulted.

As the months rolled on, my list of bizarre health symptoms only continued to increase. From insomnia, hair loss, and painful periods, to acid reflux, brain fog, extreme temperature sensitivity, chronic back and pelvic pain, excessive weight gain (over 25kgs in seven years), iron deficiency and allergic reactions to food/common household products, it was hard to keep up. One night, I found myself on my hands and knees in the bathroom of a swanky Melbourne restaurant — all because of an allergic reaction to *ginger*! Oh, and on top of all of this, my incontinence was now so severe and urgent that my bladder would sometimes empty itself without any notice!

By this stage I was becoming really frightened, and the defensive nature of every doctor I tried to speak to only worsened my anxiety. I was that one patient who kept demanding answers — which they couldn't give — and in the process, it felt like I had become 'the enemy.' With an ever-growing sense of despair, I reached out to my trusted GP of 10 years, hoping for an answer; desperately seeking some empathy and understanding. At his wit's end, he advised me I simply needed to 'see a psychiatrist.' Can you imagine how this felt, as someone who had worked in mental health for over 20 years? It was devastating! Here I was, a health-conscious, educated woman from a medical family, with a list of symptoms that no doctor could give any answers for. I felt as though they thought I was crazy.

Eventually, at age 41, I made a decision to pack up and move to Bali in an attempt to give myself a relaxing environment to recover from my 'exhaustion.' But as the weeks went by, nothing changed. In fact, my health continued to deteriorate further. I was still plagued by constant urinary tract infections, bronchitis, back issues, sharp pains down my legs, and other unexplained and debilitating symptoms. For two years, my health continued its steady, downward spiral, and I continued to believe I was simply burnt out. After all, the symptoms varied so much that there was no way to work out how they were all connected.

By 2015, however, I realised that there was no way this was simply clinical burnout. To be spending most of my days lying in bed, unable to work, and fighting an invisible illness that no one could diagnose, showed me the reality of the situation. I was seriously fucked.

By this stage, depression and shame had become so unshakable that all I wanted to do was hide away. Gradually, I slipped further and further into isolation. My friends tired of hearing about my unexplained symptoms, and my inability to fulfil my friendship duties.

My beautiful boys, now teenagers, no longer recognised their engaged and loving mother in that state. My husband had already left and my boys followed suit.

In a short period of time, I lost everyone close to me. My career was gone, and all I had left were my mounting medical bills. I wondered if this was how I was going to die.

One of the worst things about mesh is that it slowly poisons your body. You know you're dying, but no one will take you seriously. You know that something is seriously wrong, but getting a diagnosis is near impossible. It's like having a ticking time bomb in your vagina.

I tried so many things in my quest to find the truth. I even went to a tropical diseases unit in London. But no doctor could find a solution (or perhaps, none were willing to take my complaints seriously). I spent thousands of dollars with naturopaths, trying to find answers, but this only kept a few of the symptoms at bay.

It was only after my mother's funeral in 2016, that I had the mental 'space' to look into what I *could* do for my worsening incontinence — starting with going back to see my implanting surgeon. (It had been seven years since my surgery, and yet my incontinence was worse than ever!) So, plucking up the courage to once again demand answers from a doctor, I made an appointment with my surgeon and fronted him with the truth. "What is going on?" I asked. "This was supposed to fix my incontinence, and yet it's never been worse. Also, I now have all these other health issues!" As I stood there demanding answers, I realised with frightening clarity that he knew exactly what was going on. It was almost as if I could see the cogs in his mind ticking over. *Oh my God, it's one of them...*

"Sorry Justine I'm not able to help you right now, you'll have to see my colleague," he replied defensively. He couldn't get me out of the room fast enough. That was when the fear began creeping into my stomach; the realisation that something was definitely wrong.

The next red flag was when the second doctor told me he would be performing a simple urine test — but then proceeded to numb my vagina and insert a probe into my urethra. My third red flag came moments later, when I looked up at the ultrasound screen and saw his face drop like a ton of bricks.

Immediately, I reached across and grabbed the screen, tilting it toward me. There, for the first time, I saw the truth. The whole screen was awash with blue and white...

My urethra was being skewered by the mesh.

With haste, I was hurried into a cold room, where I was left traumatised and shaking in my gown for 45 minutes. You know when you're in shock and people are talking, but it feels like you're only getting every third word? That's how it felt. I had no idea what was going on, but somewhere amidst the mutterings of the doctor, I'd heard the words 'class action' and 'adverse effects' mentioned. That was enough to show me that there was something big going on; something much bigger than just me.

When the doctor returned, he looked at me soberly and gave me my prognosis. "The only option we have is to remove the mesh — but there are no guarantees. Even if I can remove every piece, it will take multiple surgeries, and you may require a permanent catheter for the rest of your life," he stated. Looking at the diagram of my 'skewered' urethra, I almost vomited. Then I was sent home.

In my traumatised state, it took a week for the gravity of the situation to sink in. *Multiple surgeries? No guarantee of successful removal? A catheter for the rest of my life?* I was 47, for Christ's sake. Surely this couldn't be the only option.

Overnight, I fell apart. I literally lost my mind. I was just so sick of being sick, and now that I'd found a 'solution' (which wasn't even a guaranteed solution), I just couldn't deal with life anymore. To know that my best-case scenario was life with a permanent catheter, was devastating. To live life from bed and not be able to walk 100 metres at a time, or stand for more than five minutes, was no kind of 'life.'

So, on one night in August 2017, I made my suicide attempt. Truly, I should not have survived that night, but I owe my life to the actions of one of my friends — one of the few who hadn't given up on me. On that night, unable to reach me by phone and knowing how fragile I was, she rushed to my house and broke down the door. I am alive today because of her intuition and selflessness in that moment; a moment in time that has since shown me that even in our darkest hours, there is always someone who still cares.

Despite going to the depths of despair and hopelessness, despite attempting to end my life, a flicker of hope had been ignited. And so, turning to Google, I began to research everything I could about pelvic mesh — eventually coming across the Australian Mesh Injured Support Group. That was the first moment I felt like I wasn't alone.

Through my research I discovered there were thousands of other women fighting this same battle — all the way from Europe and the United States, to as far as Sweden. Not only that, but many of them were travelling to the United States for mesh removal. I soon discovered that those who underwent surgery in Australia had vastly different stories to share than those who made the journey overseas. While the latter were getting their life back, not one of the women who reported undergoing surgery in Australia were sure if they'd had a partial or complete removal. They too, had paid a hefty financial sum for their surgeries, but they didn't speak well of their experiences. There appeared to be an atrocious lack of empathy for women here in Australia, and zero accountability by the medical profession, the TGA, or our government. All the while, women were continuing to lose their lives.

In October 2017, I turned to an American surgeon named Dr Dionysios Veronikis, in an attempt to save my life. In all honesty, the treatment, odds, and transparency overseas seemed like a better option. They were offering full mesh removals and Dr Veronikis had solid evidence of performing over 2000 successful surgeries. I realised that this was my only option if I wanted to continue living. So, almost $50,000 later — after liquidating my remaining possessions — I travelled alone to the United States and underwent surgery. For a device that took 20 minutes to implant, it took over eight hours to remove. As a friend of mine so eloquently said when she saw the photos of my vagina pre and post-removal surgery: "Even Blind Freddy could see that shit was killing you!"

Although my body didn't recover immediately, over a period of around 12 months, my health began to return with much work. Since my mesh removal, my chronic back and pelvic pain has reduced from a 24/7 experience to only rearing its head on certain days. No longer do I suffer from fluid retention, acid reflux, or allergies. My brain fog has cleared, my hair has grown back, and my periods are regular and normal. I can walk, function, and speak to audiences about my journey. I now have drastically improved quality of life.

However, I still live with Hashimoto's thyroid disease, chronic fatigue, nerve pain, acute anxiety disorder, and PTSD. I'm also pre-diabetic and still live with some incontinence. Interestingly, as my doctor has confirmed, I have no family history of any of these things. Just let that sink in…

For many other women, however, life after transvaginal mesh surgery is very different. Tragically, not all of us recover. Some women die from post-surgery complications and several women I know have died by their own hands, simply because they have been left with no hope, and no options for quality of life. What is abundantly clear, is that women, mothers, aunts, and daughters around the world are suffering. I have spoken to women as young as 29, right through to women in their 70's. They're missing out on playing with their children and grandkids. They're depressed. They're isolated. Their marriages are breaking down due to a lack of sexual intimacy and financial hardship. *How and why was this allowed to happen to so many women!?*

I'm still watching my 'life movie' play out. I don't know if I'll one day be able to live pain-free, enjoy pleasurable sex, and live as a fully-functioning member of society. I don't know if one day, I'll have the luxury of feeling just a little carefree; to not have to worry about my future and all I've lost, or the damage inflicted on my poor body. But I'm grateful to have some of my life back.

Remaining well is a constant battle, and I am continually learning new ways to look after myself. I know that my mental health and wellbeing are crucial to my physical recovery, and there's no 'quick fix.' After all, healing is an inside job and it's never finished.

Most weeks I do talk therapy, and I also combine the positives of antidepressant medication with natural tools like meditation. I spend lots of time in nature and choose to fill my brain with good movies, soul food, and positive stories from people who've transformed their lives too (Malala Yousafzai is one of my heroes). For me, the ocean is one of my true 'life loves', and often I'll just sit and watch the waves ebb and flow, marvelling at how much the sea mimics our own mental health journeys. Some days the waves crash hard upon us, while others there is barely a ripple in sight.

As a group of mesh-injured women, we often feel like outsiders. When it comes to something like cancer, everyone knows what it is; everyone understands it as a health issue. You get support, empathy, a diagnosis for treatment, and prognosis for the future. So often however, mesh-survivors are made to feel like we're the enemy — yet we don't want to be. We *want* to work collaboratively with the medical industry and governments; we want to make sure this never happens again. But we need support. We need empathy. We need acknowledgement that something terrible happened to us. Whether on purpose or accidentally, our lives were ruined, and we need that acknowledgment.

Knowing what I know now, I understand why so many women disengage from medical help; how it feels to be made to believe you're going crazy. All of this needs to be kept in mind when treating someone with mesh injury. We are damaged. We react negatively. We are very scared, sick, and in a lot of pain. And that can cause bad behaviour in any human being.

I count myself as one of the lucky ones. I'm able to work, and I have significantly less pain than I was once living with. I've since become the President and Co-Founder of 'Mesh Injured Australia' and am working alongside the Royal Prince Alfred Hospital to co-design a pelvic mesh clinic in Sydney. Taking on this next chapter of my life meant leaving Bali and relocating back to Sydney, but I've never felt surer of anything in my life.

As a society, it's not really seen as socially acceptable to talk about things like incontinence (much less, vaginas!); but I hope that by being so open with my journey, it will help the loved ones of mesh-injured women to understand with more empathy what we are dealing with; to stay by our side and fight with us. Because it's a long journey, and we need you. Whether it's physical or mental pain, every human needs someone by their side during tough times. *Please*, don't give up on us.

> *JUSTINE WATSON is the President and Co-founder of Mesh Injured Australia, and has more than two decades of experience as a mental healthcare worker. As a survivor of pelvic mesh surgery, she is passionate about educating medical professionals about the damage of mesh, and the realities faced by survivors and their families. Based in Sydney (Australia) she now works alongside professionals at the Royal Prince Alfred Hospital to provide consumer co-design to a multi-disciplinary clinic for survivors of pelvic mesh implants. Find out more about Justine's work at meshinjuredaustralia.org.au*

RESOURCES

"If you are struggling, please don't suffer alone. Please don't go into this bubble where your friends don't know that they need to be there for you. There's no shame in reaching out. We're all human, we all go through shit, and we all need help sometimes."

— Jas Rawlinson

Get the Facts

What is depression?

Depression is more than just feeling sad or low during tough times. People with depression can have intense negative feelings for weeks, months or even years, sometimes for no good reason.

Depression is relatively common, affecting more than one million Australians each year. Unfortunately, many people with depression don't recognise it or get help — but it is treatable and most people with depression go on to lead happy, productive lives with the right treatment for them.

Possible causes of depression

- Relationship problems or conflict – e.g. separation/divorce, difficult/abusive relationship.
- Job loss, especially long-term unemployment.
- Loneliness or feeling isolated.
- Excessive drug or alcohol use.
- Having another family member who has depression.
- Having a serious physical illness.
- Changes in how the brain functions.
- Personality factors – e.g. anxiety, low self-esteem.

Causes of depression vary from person to person because of a mix of personal risk factors and difficult life events. It's also common for people to experience depression and anxiety at the same time.

Signs of depression
- Feeling sad, 'flat' or down most of the time (for two weeks or more).
- Losing interest in activities you used to enjoy (for two weeks or more).
- Feeling tired or lacking energy and motivation.
- Moodiness that is out of character.
- Increased irritability and frustration.
- Increased alcohol and drug use.
- Changes in your weight or appetite.
- Having problems sleeping or sleeping all the time.
- Feeling worthless or guilty.
- Feeling restless, edgy or slowed down.
- Having difficulty concentrating or making decisions.
- Thinking repeatedly about death or suicide.

If you are experiencing a number of these symptoms, you may have depression. It is very important to visit your GP or another health professional for a full assessment and to discuss treatment options.

Helpful tips for addressing depression
Taking steps to manage depression is important for your current and long-term health. Depression is an illness that can get worse if left untreated.
1. See your doctor—talk to your doctor about how you've been feeling to find the most appropriate treatment for you. Your doctor can also refer you to a psychologist or other mental health professional for treatment, sometimes with a rebate through Medicare.
2. Talk to someone you trust—talking to family, friends, a counsellor, minister, or a crisis line, can help you develop an understanding of your situation and help you move forward. There

are some very effective treatments through psychologists/ mental health professionals that can make a real difference.
3. Look after yourself—eat a balanced diet, exercise regularly, and get enough sleep. Exercise has been shown to help reduce depression. Take time out to relax and do things you used to enjoy, even if you don't feel like it now. When you have depression, it can be hard to get motivated, but it's important not to isolate yourself.
4. Be aware of your feelings—noticing changes in your mood and thoughts, and identifying what situations make you feel good and bad, can help to stop negative thought patterns.
5. Keep safe—you may be having thoughts about dying and feel that it may be better to 'not be around,' or feel that you don't know how much longer you can go on. These thoughts are common when people feel very depressed. If you have these thoughts, get help straight away.

About suicide

Suicide is the leading cause of death for Australians aged between 15 and 44. Men are four times more likely to die by suicide than women, and ABS data (2012) shows more people die from suicide than road deaths.

Most people don't want to die, they just want their pain to stop.

Everyone has a role to play in preventing suicide; choices we make today can help prevent suicide.

Why does someone consider suicide?

Life can be painful and problems can seem overwhelming at times. Some people may think about suicide but do not act upon it. For others, suicide seems like the only way out of their situation or the feelings they are experiencing. They generally feel very alone and hopeless. They believe nobody can help them or understand what they are going through.

There are many reasons why someone considers suicide:
- Relationship break-ups.
- Family problems.
- Sexual, physical or emotional abuse.
- Drug or alcohol problems.
- Mental illness, including schizophrenia, bipolar disorder and depression.
- Eating disorders like Anorexia.
- Major loss and grief, such as a death or the suicide of a friend, family member, public figure.
- School, uni or work problems.
- Unemployment or being unemployed for a long time.
- Feeling like they don't belong anywhere.
- Financial or legal problems.
- Any problem that they can't see a solution for.

Almost everyone who takes their own life gives some clue or warning. Never ignore suicide threats. Take people's suicidal thoughts and feelings very seriously and help them find effective help.

Possible signs someone might be thinking about suicide

Most suicidal individuals give warning signs or signals of their intentions. The best way to prevent suicide is to recognise these warning signs and respond to them.

Feelings:
- Hopelessness.
- Feeling trapped.
- Depression.
- Irritable/moody, angry.
- Worthlessness.
- No sense of purpose/reason for living.

Situations:
- Previous suicide attempts.
- Talking or writing about suicide/death, even if it seems to be a joke.
- Seeking access to something they can kill themselves with.
- Being moody, withdrawn, or sad.
- Saying goodbye/giving away possessions.
- Losing interest in things they previously enjoyed.
- Taking less care of their appearance.
- Anxiety or agitation, including difficulty concentrating or sleeping.
- Engaging in self-destructive or risky behaviour.
- Increased use of alcohol or drugs.
- Withdrawal from other people.
- Sometimes a positive mood after a period of being down may indicate the person has made up their mind to take their own life and feels relief that the decision has been made.

3 Steps to help prevent suicide

1. Ask.
If you think someone might be suicidal, ask them directly: "Are you thinking about suicide?" Don't be afraid to do this, it shows you care, and will actually decrease their risk because it shows someone is willing to talk about it. Make sure you ask directly and unambiguously.

2. Listen and stay with them.
If they say 'yes', they are suicidal, listen to them and allow them to express how they are feeling. Don't leave them alone. Stay with them or get someone else reliable to stay with them.

3. Get help.
Get them appropriate help. Call a crisis line or 000 if the person's life is in danger. If you can get in straight away visit a GP or psychologist.

Even if the danger is not immediate, they may need longer-term support for the issues that led to them feeling this way.

Be aware that in some situations a person may refuse help—remember, you cannot force someone to get assistance. Instead, focus on ensuring the appropriate people are aware of the situation. Don't shoulder this responsibility yourself.

Many thanks to Lifeline for providing the above information.

Jas Rawlinson's Hand-Picked Mental Health Warriors

Over the past two years, I've met with many amazing grassroots organisations and individuals who are changing lives through the power of storytelling, community meetups, and professional services. I've witnessed many of these legends working just as hard — if not more so — than some of the big organisations, and with far less funding.

Below are some of my mental health warrior friends; everyday people with lived experience of mental health challenges, who spend every day spreading awareness, breaking down stigma, saving lives, and providing unwavering support to their communities.

REDSIX

Founded by Australian Army veteran Michael Handley, REDSIX is a user-friendly app that aims to lower Aussie veteran suicide rates. Offering 24/7 peer support for over 200 veterans a week, the app has already received support from numerous celebrities, including James Stewart (Home & Away) and Daniel MacPherson (Bad Mothers/Neighbours), and has already saved lives. Features of the app include a daily 'mood tracker' (users can select a green, amber, red, or black button), GPS technology (allowing users to discover and meet with others in their area), and the ability to trigger support from emergency services if a user is at risk. As explained by Michael: "Black means you are at risk of self-harm and need to speak with a professionally trained counsellor, who will then make an assessment as to whether or not emergency services need to be alerted, and can attend their location for a mental health check. Likewise, when

'Red' is pushed, a direct alert is sent to three 'battle buddies' (who have been programmed in by the user upon registration) who will then receive a text message with a button they can push to call the user. If these three users are unable to make contact, the at-risk user will be diverted back to the main area, where users within their set GPS radius can touch base and offer to go for a coffee or walk, or just offer to lend an ear."

W: redsix.com.au

Mindfull Aus

Founded in 2016 by Matt Runnalls, Mindfull Aus is a not-for-profit foundation dedicated to 'taking a youthful, realistic, and comfortable approach to talking about mental illness, wellness, and suicide.' Through regular facilitations around Australia from compassionate, lived-experience advocates with inspiring journeys of hope, healing, and recovery, their aim is to foster deep community connection, and empower individuals to take acceptance and onus for their wellbeing.

W: mindfullaus.org

Kick On

Based in Australia, Kick On is a registered charity promoting positive mental health and wellbeing through unique programs aimed toward both men and women, as well as FIFO workers and primary/high school students. Through their Kick On clothing brand, they empower everyday community members to become mental health ambassadors, and to create support networks within their communities.

W: www.kickon.com.au

Youth Wellbeing Project

In recent years, reports have emerged of children being exposed to explicit digital content as young as five years of age — statistically, as many as 3 in 4 boys and 1 in 4 girls access pornography under the age of 13. Without intervention, many young people are modelling their ideas toward sex and relationships entirely from porn (which can lead to devastating social, mental and relational outcomes). For reasons such as these, it's never been more important for schools, communities and parents to be aware of organisations who offer innovative solutions and training to help counteract the impact of our increasingly hypersexualised culture. One of my favourite organisations is Youth Wellbeing Project — a grassroots community organisation who work across Australia, and internationally, to positively impact youth sexuality and wellbeing through age-appropriate programs and resources that help young people make sense of images they see online or through the media. To find out more about their workshops, presentations, and school programs, visit:

W: youthwellbeingproject.com.au

Dion Jensen

As a former police officer and soldier who now works as a corporate speaker and trainer, Dion Jensen understands intricately the mental health challenges faced by millions around the world. Based from New Zealand and Singapore, Dion now travels around the world helping individuals, organisations, and communities to understand their 'Value, Identity and Purpose' (The VIP of Mental Health), while providing innovative solutions on everything from corporate bullying and mental health issues, to increasing engagement, productivity, and revenue. Always humble, Dion knows his lived-experience is crucial to his ability to help change lives, and says he could not have achieved this level of success without first going through the darkness.

W: dionjensen.com

Professional Support Contacts

If you or someone you know are struggling with feelings of depression, anxiety, or hopelessness, please contact one of the following. There is always someone who cares and is ready to listen.

Lifeline

For 24/7 crisis support and suicide prevention services, call Lifeline on 13 11 14, or use their online chat every night from 7pm at lifeline.org.au/crisischat.

W: lifeline.org.au

Beyond Blue

P: 1300 22 4636 **W:** beyondblue.org.au

Kids Helpline

P: 1800 551 800 **W:** kidshelpline.com.au

Suicide Call Back Service

P: 1300 659 467 **W:** suicidecallbackservice.org.au

Mates4Mates

P: 1300 462 837 **W:** mates4mates.org

Mensline
P: 1300 78 99 78 W: mensline.org.au

1800 Respect
P: 1800 737 732 W: 1800respect.org.au

White Wreath
Call or text with a real person (Monday-Friday, 5am - 9pm).
Ph. 1300 766 177 / 0410 526 562 W: whitewreath.org.au

Acknowledgements

As I sit here writing the final words for the second volume of 'Reasons to Live,' it blows my mind to think of how far this project has come. From a tiny spark of thought back in 2016, to what has now become a book series read and reviewed around the world, it's still crazy for me to think of how much things can change in just a few short years!

Once again, I have to start by thanking my entire family. Thank you for listening to all my ideas, putting up with my constant talk about suicide prevention (not always an easy topic to talk about), coming together to babysit when I'm off at events, and giving me the emotional and physical support needed to actually get this book written. You are all such a blessing in my life, and I couldn't do this work without you!

To my husband Chris: you've put up with me being attached to my laptop and phone pretty much every day for the past year, while growing my business and writing this book, and that has meant we don't always get a lot of time together. Thank you for choosing to be supportive and gracious, even when it comes with sacrifice.

Selena Soo — though we've never met, your coaching and business support has changed my life 110%. Without your incredible knowledge and guidance, I'm not sure this book would have happened! Thank you for inspiring me with your absolutely kick-ass entrepreneurial advice, and always encouraging me with my ideas.

To my publisher, Ocean Reeve, thank you once again for helping me bring my message to the world!

Kevin Hines — thank you for being so gracious with your time and giving me your heartfelt advice and direction earlier this year when I started to let the naysayers get in my ear. You gave me the final push I needed to level up, strap on my warrior suit, and release these stories as they are. You are an absolute gem in this world! PS. Hurry up and get back to Aus for a visit!

To my friends at Royal Flying Doctor Service QLD, thank you for supporting and sponsoring several of my events over the past year. I couldn't get my message out to as many people as I have, without your financial and heartfelt support.

And finally, thank you to my entire 'Reasons to Live tribe.' (Yes, that's you!) I wrote this for you, and every other person out there who is in need of hope, guidance, encouragement, and inspiration. Together, we are stronger, and the fact that you are reading this book is a gift I will always struggle to fully comprehend. Thank you for giving your time to read this book.

Author Bio
Jas Rawlinson

Jas Rawlinson is an Australian mental health speaker, memoir writing coach, and the author of the series 'Reasons to Live: One More Day, Every Day.'

As a survivor of family violence and sexual assault, Jas is highly regarded for her sensitivity when reporting on taboo topics and is often requested to speak on social issues including mental health, domestic violence, and human trafficking.

She has spent time in Thailand with sex trafficking survivors and undercover rescue workers, and in 2016 received national media coverage for co-founding Brisbane's first permanent domestic violence memorial.

Published both nationally and internationally, Jas has written many trending news articles, with several reaching over 100K people in their first 48 hours. She has also been featured across ABC News, 9 News, News.com.au and Daily Mail, and has had her work endorsed by high-profile names such as Kevin Hines, Lifeline Hunter Valley, Royal Flying Doctor Service QLD, Project Karma, and Women's Legal Service QLD.

She is based in both Brisbane and Coffs Harbour, and is available for speaking engagements, author mentoring, and ghostwriting assignments worldwide.

Connect with Jas

Have you always wanted to write your own book, but don't know where to start?

Looking for an engaging event speaker to talk on issues of mental health, domestic violence, or human trafficking?

Keen to get another copy of 'Reasons to Live?'

Jump on www.jasrawlinson.com to connect.

@jas_rawlinson

@jas_rawlinson

Reasons to Live One More Day, Every Day

thoughtsfromjas.com

www.ingramcontent.com/pod-product-compliance
Lightning Source LLC
Chambersburg PA
CBHW071452080526
44587CB00014B/2078